Daniel Brink Towner

Towner's Male Choir

Daniel Brink Towner

Towner's Male Choir

ISBN/EAN: 9783337296506

Printed in Europe, USA, Canada, Australia, Japan

Cover: Foto ©Thomas Meinert / pixelio.de

More available books at **www.hansebooks.com**

Towner's Male Choir

Nos. 1, 2, 3, 4
(Combined)

By D. B. Towner

Chicago   New York   Toronto

Fleming H. Revell Company

London   Edinburgh

PUBLISHERS' PREFACE

The cordial appreciation accorded parts 1 and 2 of Towner's Male Choir and the popular demand for a more comprehensive volume of praise for male voices has induced author and publisher to issue the present volume, believing it to be a most helpful accessory in the service of praise, more especially for Y. M. C. A., Y. P. S. C. E. and Evangelistic meetings.

In its convenient pocket size it will, we confidently expect, occupy a large field of usefulness.

MAKE JESUS KING.

Written for the student's foreign missionary movement of the American Intercollegiate Young Men's Association, Northfield Mass., 1888.

E. BROCK.   CARL WILHELM. Arr. D. B. T.

1. Make Da-vid king! that watch-word thrilled; Make David king! that
2. Make Je-sus king! why long-er stay? Make Je-sus king! for
3. Make Je-sus king! keep rank, keep rank! Make Je-sus king! the
4. Make Je-sus king! each stal-wart band; Make Je-sus king! from

pur-pose filled, The hosts those might-y cap-tains bring, To
day by day There comes to help Him, at His word, A
riv-er bank Stopped not those men of Da-vid's host. We're
all the land Let ev-'ry tribe its trib-ute bring And

make their glorious leader king. Thine, Thine are we, and on Thy side. Who
great host, like the host of God. Thine, Thine are we, and on Thy side. Our
marshalled by the Ho-ly Ghost. Thine, Thine are we, and on Thy side. We
haste to make the Savior King. Thine, Thine are we, and at Thy side, We

for our sins was cru-ci-fied! To make Thee King in-deed o'er
weakness to Thy strength al-lied, To make Thee King, we come with
fear not Jordan's swell-ing tide, To make Thee King, be-yond the
would in fel-low-ship a-bide, To make Thee King, we need Thy

4

MAKE JESUS KING.

all this world. We now Thy roy-al ban-ner have un-furled.
joy to - day. To give Thy peaceful scep-tre boundless sway.
wid - est sea, To dis - tant lands we glad-ly fol - low Thee.
Spir - it's power, Oh, con-se-crate us whol-ly from this hour.

WE'RE ON THE WAY.

S. M. SAYFORD.   D. B. TOWNER.

1. The promised land! by faith I see, Where God' own glo - ry
2. The promised land! where thousands dwell, Who've washed their robes in
3. The promised land! with mansions fair, Where Je - sus now pre -
4. The promised land! the Fa - ther's house, A - waits us on the

gilds the day, Where we shall dwell with Christ re-deemed, By
Je - sus' blood, With them we'll wave the branch of palm, When
pares a place, From whence He'll come to take us home, And
shin- ing shore. When there we'll strike our harps of gold, And

CHORUS.

His own grace We're on the way.
we have crossed the nar - row flood.   } We're on the way, we're
we shall see Him face to face.
praise His name for - ev - ermore.

ou the way; To glo - ry - land, we're on the way; We fol - low

Je - sus, day by day; He leads us all a - long the way.

WE ARE GOING HOME.

N. B. S.

Moderato.

N. B. SARGENT, Arr.

1. We are sailing to-day on the o - cean of life, Where the billows are
2. It is gloom - y night on the rag - ing tide, But brightly will
3. There's a beautiful land be - yond the sea, A cit - y that's

dash - ing high, We are tempest-toss'd a-mid scenes of strife, And
break the morn, And we know our Cap-tain will safe-ly guide Our
bright and fair, Where sin and sor - row can nev - er be; And

CHORUS.

dan - gers are ev - er nigh. But we are go - ing home, we are
bark thro' the wild - est storm. So we are go - ing home, we are
dear ones a - wait us there. Oh! we are go - ing home, we are

go - ing home, We are nearing the shin - ing shore. ... Of the
heavenly shore

land that is fair - er, where joys are pur - er, And our journey will

soon be o'er, We are go - ing home, go - ing home, go - ing
go - ing, go - ing

WE ARE GOING HOME.

f   *p*   *Rall.*

home... We are go-ing home, going home, go - ing home.

going, go-ing home.

going home,   go - ing home.

ABLE TO SAVE.

Rev. J. H. SAMMIS.   J. H. TENNEY. Arr by D B T

1. Par - don in Je - sus, my brother, All who will seek Him may
2. Ful - ly the sin that I brought Him He in His kind-ness for -
3. If we re-pent, there's re - mis - sion, This is the prom - ise He
4. Come to Him now, and, re - ceiv - ing Free-ly the bless-ing you

is

have; Tho' there is help in none oth - er Je - sus is a - ble, to
gave, All who for mer cy have sought Him, Je - sus is a - ble, to
gave, Hearts that are moved with contri-tion, Je - sus is a - ble to
crave, Trust and con-fess Him, be - liev - ing Je - sus is a - ble, to

a - ble to save. CHORUS.

A-ble to save,   a-ble to save,

save...... A - ble to save,...... a - ble to save,......

A-ble to save,   a-ble to save,

Jesus is a - blo and willing to save,....   Able to save,....
is able and willing to save,   Able to save,

a-ble to save,......   Je-sus is a - ble and willing to save.
a-ble to save,

GO, LABOR ON.

W. H. PONTIUS. By per.

1. Go, la - bor on, while it is day; The world's dark night is
2. Men die in dark-ness at your side, With - out a hope to
3. Toil on, faint not; keep watch and pray: Be wise the err-ing
4. Go, la - bor on, your bands are weak; Your knees are faint, your

bast'ning on; Speed, speed thy work—cast sloth a - way! It
cheer the tomb; Take up the torch and wave it wide—The
soul to win: Go forth . in - to the world's highway; Com-
soul cast down, Yet fal - ter not; the prize you seek Is

GO, LABOR ON.

CHORUS.

is not thus that souls are won. La-bor on. . . . . . . while
torch that lights time's thickest gloom.
pel the wan-d'rer to come in.
near,—a king-dom and a crown. Go, la-bor on, while

it is day, (while it is day,) Go, la bor on, Speed thy

work,. . . . . cast sloth a - way; Go, la - bor on.
Speed, speed thy work,

COME, SPIRIT, COME.

Mrs. HARRIET JONES.

D. B. TOWNER.

Andante.

1. Come, Spir-it, come, . . with light di-vine! . . . . . Il - lu-mi-
2. Dear Sav-ior, be. . . . . . . my constant guide, ... My ev - er
3. A strong-er faith. . . . . . is my de - sire,. . . . . . . A nearness,

1. Come, Spir-it, come, with light di-vine! Il-
2. Dear Sav-ior, be my constant guide, My
3 A strong-er faith, is my de - sire, A

Copyright. 1883. by D. B. Towner

nate..... my soul;...... Come soothe and cheer.. this heart of
pres - - ent friend;.... Oh, keep me near.... Thy bleeding
Lord,.... to Thee;...... Oh, send just now.... the ho - ly

In- ot- nate my wait-ing soul;   Come soothe and cheer   this
ev - er pres- ent, lov - ing friend;   Oh, keep me near   Thy
nearness, blessed Lord, to Thee;   Oh, send just now   the

Ad lib.

mine,...... And ev -'ry foe......... con - trol...:...
side...... Till all the strife...... shall end......
fire,...... To ev - er dwell.. .... in me......

heart of mine,   And ev -'ry in - ward foe con - trol.
bleed-ing side   Till all the toil and strife shall end.
ho - ly fire,   To ev - er sweet-ly dwell in me.

CHORUS.

Come, Spir-it, come, with light di - vine, De - scend, O heav'nly

Dove, Shine in un-til this heart of mine Is all a - glow with love.

COMRADES IN BATTLE.

C. B. COMFORT.   D. B. TOWNER.

1. Comrades in bat-tle, Sol-diers of Je-sus! Trumpets are sounding for
2. Comrades in bat-tle, Close up the column; For-ward along the whole
3. Comrades in bat-tle, True to each oth-er, Shoulder to shoulder fight
4. Comrades in bat-tle, Wounded and bleeding, Angels are close by your
5. Comrades in bat-tle, Joy-ful the wel-come, Wait-ing to greet you on

war, (press onward) Foe - men are gath-'ring, fierce for the con - flict,
line, (press forward) Charge the foe bold - ly; cour-age, ye brave ones;
on, (press forward) Loy - al and lov - ing; brother, with broth-er,
side, (press forward) Up to the Fa - ther, swift-ly they're lead-ing
high, (press forward) An - gels shall crown you, loved ones surround you,

CHORUS.

An - gels are wait-ing in awe. ⎞
Lift up the cross for your sign   ⎟
Christ in the heart of each one. ⎬ Comrades in battle, forward for Jesus,
Souls that for Je-sus have died. ⎟
Je-sus shall bid you come nigh. ⎠ Forward, forward, forward for Jesus,

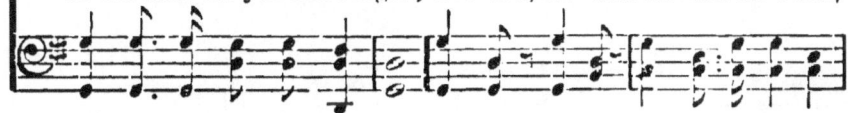

Hark to His stir-ring command. (press forward) gazing from glo ry,

think how He sees us, For - ward, for-ward, ye conquering band.

THE RICHES OF LOVE.

Rev. H. B. Hartzler.   N. B. Sargent. Arr.

1. The treas-ures of earth are not mine, I hold not its sil - ver and
2. The treas-ures of earth must all fail, Its rich-es and hon - or de-
3. Compared with the rich - es of love, The wealth of the world is but
4. Come, take of the rich - es of Christ, Ex-haust-less, and free is the

gold: But a treas-ure far great-er is mine; I have rich-es of
cay, But the rich - es of love that are mine, Even death can not
dross, I will seek but Christ Je-sus to win, And for Him I count
store, Of its won - der - ful full-ness receive, Till you hunger and

CHORUS.

val - ue un - told.
take them a - way. } Oh, the depths of the riches of love,...... The
all things but loss.   the riches of love,
thirst nev - er - more.

rich-es of love in Christ Je - sus, Far bet-ter than gold, or

wealth un-told, Are the rich-es of love in Christ Je— sus.

GIVE ME THY HEART.

Rev. J. H. Sammis   D. B. Towner.

1. To thee, who from the nar-row road, In sin-ful ways so long have
2. Ah, well that gen-tle voice I know, For oft it called me long a-
3. "My son!" oh, word of might-y grace, That children of our mortal
4. How great that Fa-ther's love must be, How fond His yearnings after
5. How pa-tient hath His spir-it been, To fol-low thee thro' all thy
6. O God, my Fa-ther! I o-bey; I come, I come to Thee to-

trod, How kind-ly speaks thy Father, God, "My son, give Me thy heart."
go, And now to thee it whis-pers low, "My son, give Me thy heart."
race With sons of God may take their place, "My son, give Me thy heart."
thee, That He should say so ten-der-ly, "My son, give Me thy heart."
sin, And plead, Thy way-ward soul to win, "My son, give Me thy heart."
day, "Here Lord, I give my-self a-way, I give to Thee my heart!"

CHORUS.

"My son,   my son,   give me   thy
Give Me thy heart,   give Me thy heart,   My son, give Me thy

heart,   Oh, hear and heed thy Fa-ther's call, And give to Him thy heart.
(*Last verse.*) I hear and heed my Fa-ther's call, And give to Him my heart.
heart, give Me thy heart,

THE WHOLE WIDE WORLD FOR JESUS.

KATHARINE H. JOHNSON.   D. B. TOWNER.

1. The whole wide world for Je - sus! Once more, be-fore we part,
2. The whole wide world for Je - sus! From out the Gold-en Gate,
3. The whole wide world for Je - sus! Its hearts, and homes, and thrones,

Ring out the joy-ful watch-word From ev - 'ry grate-ful heart.
Thro' all the South Sea is - lands, To Chi - na's princely state;
Ring out a - gain the watch-word In loud and joy - ous tones;

Let ev 'ry voice be ea - ger To swell the glad re frain,
F'rom In - dia's vales and mount-ains, Thro' Per-sia's land of bloom,
The whole wide world for Je - sus! With pray'r the song we'll sing,

And ev - 'ry soul be val-iant The world for Christ to gain.
To sto - ried Pal - es - ti - na And Af - ric's des ert gloom.
And speed the pray'r with la- bor, Till earth shall crown Him King.

CHORUS.

The whole wide world for Je - sus! Be this our bat - tle cry;

The Cru - ci - fied shall con - quer, And vic - to ry is nigh.

16 CLING TO THE BIBLE, MY BOY.

WILL S. HAYES. ARR.

D. B. TOWNER.

Declamando.

ORGAN.

1. As your journey, thro' life to the grave, you pur-sue, There is
2. You may meet with misfor-tune and sor-rows and tears, You may
3. Put your faith in our Fa-ther and you will be strong, Keep your
4. Ev-'ry time that you read it, you'll learn something new, Of
5. 'Tis the anch-or of hope, and the lamp that gives light, 'Tis the.

one thing in earn-est I wish you to do, Oh, list-en, my
bat-tle with sin and with Sa-tan for years, Be a Christian, press
eye on the cross and you'll nev-er go wrong, Sing the sweet songs of
Je-sus who died on the cross to save you, To the Lord, to your-
star that will shine thro' your life's darkest night, If you fol-low its

boy, while I say this to you,—Oh, cling to the Bi-ble, my
on, do not have an-y fears, But cling to the Bi-ble, my
praise as you jour-ney a-long,—And cling to the Bi-ble, my
self, and to heav-en be true, And cling to the Bi-ble, my
guidance you'll al-ways be right, Oh, cling to the Bi-ble, my

CHORUS.

boy.. * Then cling to the Bi-ble, my boy, ... Oh,

the Bi ble, my boy,

cling to the Bi-ble, my boy,..... While liv-ing, or dying, all

the Bible, my boy,

else let-ting go, Oh, cling to the Bi-ble, my boy.

When sung as a solo, take the second Tenor, using the small notes.

TRAVELING HOME.

J. CENNICK.   T C. O'KANE Arr.

1. Chil-dren of the heav'n-ly King. As we jour-ney let us sing,
2. Fear not, brethren, joy-ful stand On the bor-ders of our land,
3. Lord, o-be-dient-ly we'll go, Glad-ly leav-ing all be-low,

Copyright, 1888, by D. B. Towner.

TRAVELING HOME.

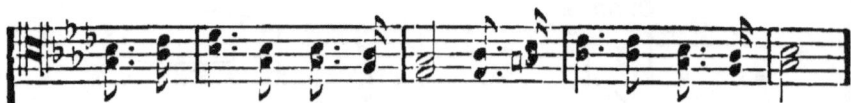

Sing our Sav-ior's wor-thy praise, Glorious in His works and ways.
Je - sus Christ, our Father's Son, Bids us un-dis-mayed go on.
On - ly Thou our lead - er be, And we still will fol - low Thee.

CHORUS.

We are trav'ling home, trav'ling home to God

We are trav - - ling home to God In the

In the narrow way, way our fathers trod, They are happy now,

way........ our fathers trod, They are hap - - - py

hap - py now, and we Soon their hap - pi - ness shall see.

now, and we Soon their hap-pi-ness shall see,

TRUST AND OBEY.

Rev. J. H. Sammis.   D. B. Towner.

1. When we walk with the Lord, In the light of His word, What a
2. Not a shad-ow can rise, Not a cloud in the skies, But His
3. Not a bur-den we bear, Not a sor row we share, But our
4. But we nev-er can prove, The de-lights of His love, Un-til
5. Then in fel-low-ship sweet, We will sit at His feet, Or we'll

glo-ry He sheds on our way; While we do His good will, He a
smile quickly drives it a-way; Not a doubt nor a fear, Not a
toil He doth rich-ly re-pay; Not a grief nor a loss, Not a
all on the al-tar we lay, For the fa-vor He shows, And the
walk by His side in the way; What He says we will do, 'Where He

bides with us still, And with all who will trust and o-bey.
sigh nor a tear, Can a-bide while we trust and o-bey.
frown nor a cross But is blest if we trust and o-bey.
joy He be-stows, Are for them who will trust and o-bey.
sends we will go, Nev-er fear, on-ly trust and o-bey.

CHORUS.

Trust and o-bey, for there's no oth-er way, To be

Copyright, 1888, by D. B. Towner.

TRUST AND OBEY.

hap - py in Je - sus, but to trust and o - bey.

HE THAT GOETH FORTH.

J. E. H.

J. E. HALL. Arr.

1. He that go - eth forth and weepeth, Bear - ing pre - cious
2. He that go - eth forth and weepeth, Trust - ing in the
3. He that go - eth forth and weepeth, All a - glow with
4. He that go - eth forth with weeping, Christ he nev - er

seed, Let him know that as he sow - eth To , the
Lord, Let him know that as he sow - eth Of the
love, Oft - en-times just while he sow - eth Hearts be-
leaves, Doubtless shall re - turn re - joic - ing! Bring-ing

CHORUS.   p   f

sin-ner's need, So he'll reap.
precious word That he'll reap.
gin to move, So he'll reap.   } Sow-ing now, sow-ing now, But
home his sheaves, Thus he'll reap.

HE THAT GOETH FORTH.

21

reap-ing by and by, Weeping now, weeping now, Re-joic-ing by and by.

THE ARMY OF REDEMPTION.

T. WHITING BANCROFT. D. B. TOWNER.

1. Will you fol - low the lead of the glo - ri - fied One, While the
2. Will you. fol - low the lead of the glo - ri - fied King? For this
3. Will you fol - low the lead of the glo - ri - fied Son, As His
4. Will you fol - low the lead of the cru - ci - fied Lord, As His

host sings His praise as they now march a-long? In the land of Ju -
Lead - er of hosts is the An-cient of Days; Will you now tune your
ar - my is march-ing to strive for the right? For the darkness is
ar - my ad - vanc-es pre-pared for the strife, With the sword of the

de - a, the march was begun, And the earth now is girdled with song.
voic-es His glo - ry to sing, As the earth now is girdled with praise
waning, the day is be-gun, And the earth now is girdled with light,
Spirit His own spoken word? All the earth now is girdled with life.

Copyright, 1893, by D. B. Towner.

CHORUS.

Sound loud!   sound loud!   the trumpet of sal-va-tion As the
Sound loud!   sound loud!

ar-my of Je-sus now marches a-long. Proclaim! proclaim!   to

ev-'ry tribe and na-tion That the whole earth is girdled with song.

LET HIM IN.

Behold, I stand at the door and knock.—Rev. 3: 10.

MRS. HARRIET JONES.   D. B. TOWNER.

1. Be - hold, a stran - ger, won-drous fair, Is knocking at   the
2. He wait-eth now—with nail-pierced hand Held out in mer - cy
3. This Friend has wait-ed there be-fore, Has oft-en knocked up-

door, my brother; The king - ly friend, that lin - gers there, Is
to   en-treat thee; Can you such ten - der love with-stand From
on   the por - tal, My broth-er, o - pen *now* the door To

CHORUS.

bet - ter far than .an - y oth - er.   } Let   Him in,
One who saves, and saves com-plete-ly?   } Hear Him knocking,
Him who bring-eth joys im - mor - tal.

let Him in,   This friend more true than *an - y* oth-er, Such
gen- tly knocking,

love thy heart should surely win; Oh! let this stranger in, my brother.

REDEEMED.

Mrs. Harriet Jones.   D. B. Towner.

1. Oh, glad "who-so-ev-er," the deed is done. My sins are
2. I came to my Sav-ior, His word be-lieved, When He the
3. Oh, glad "who-so-ev-er," the crim son tide Is free and

par-doned thro' Christ the Son, Of love so pre-cious I
sin-ner at once re-ceived, And now His prais-es I
o-pen, is deep and wide, Oh, come, my brother, and

nev-er had dreamed, Oh, sweet is the peace of the soul redeemed.
joy-ful-ly sing, And dwell in the love of my Lord and King.
bathe in the stream, And you shall be fill-ed with joy supreme.

Chorus.

Oh, glo - - ry to Je - - sus, re-deemed!......
Oh, glo-ry to Je-sus, my soul is redeemed! My soul is redeemed,

re - deemed!. .... Of love so precious I nev - er had
My soul is redeemed!

dream'd, Oh, rap - - tu - rous sto - - ry, re -
Oh, rap - tu - rous sto - ry, my soul is redeemed! My

deemed!...... re - deemed!...... Oh, glo - -
soul is redeemed! My soul is redeemed! Oh, glo - ry, Oh, glo -

ad lib.

ry, Oh, glo - ry, re - deemed!...... re - deemed!....
ry, my soul is re-deemed! My soul is redeemed! My soul is redeemed!

26 THO' YOUR SINS BE AS SCARLET.

F J. CROSBY.   W. H. DOANE.

DUET. *Gently.*

1. Tho' your sins be as scar-let, They shall be as white as snow: as snow:
2. Hear the voice that entreats you, Oh, return ye un-to God! to God!
3. He'll forgive your transgressions And remember them no more; no more;

QUARTET.

Tho' they be red............ like crimson, They shall be as wool.
He is of great.......... com-pas-sion, And of won-drous love.
Look un-to Me,............ ye peo-ple, Saith the Lord your God.

Tho' they be red,

DUET.   *p*   **QUARTET.** *f*

Tho' your sins be as scar-let, Tho' your sins be as scar-let, They shall
Hear the voice that entreats you, Hear the voice that entreats you, Oh, re-
He'll forgive your transgressions, He'll forgive your transgressions, And re-

be as white as snow, They shall be as white as snow.
turn ye un-to God! Oh, re-turn ye un-to God!
mem-ber them no more, And re-mem-ber them no more.

By permission.

WALKING WITH GOD.

27

GEORGE RAWSON.

W. H. PONTIUS.

1. Walk - ing with Thee, my God, Sav - ior be - nign,
2. Walk - ing with Thee, my God, Like as a child
3. Walk - ing with Thee, my God, Hum - bly with Thee;

Dai - ly con - fer on me Con - verse di - vine;
Leans on his fa - ther's strength, Cross - ing the wild;
Yet from all care and fear Lov - ing - ly free,

Je - sus, in Thee re - stored, Broth - er, and
And by the way is taught Les - sons of
E'en as a friend with friend, Cheer'd to the

bless - ed Lord, Let it be mine, Let it be mine.
ho - ly thought, Faith un - de - filed, Faith un - de-filed.
jour - ney's end, Walk ing with Thee, Walk - ing with Thee.

ritard.

By permission.

28 AND THE SPIRIT AND THE BRIDE.

Rev. J. H. Sammis.   D. B. Towner.

1. Ye sons of men, to you we bring Glad ti - dings from our
2. Ye souls oppressed by guilt - y fears, Ye hearts o'erwhelmed by
3. Ye doubting saints, that dare not say "I am the Lord's," be-
4. Ye peo - ple, He re - fus - eth none, Who seek His grace thro'

Lord the King, In Je - sus' great and spot-less name, To
sighs and tears, Come hith - er to the mer cy - seat, To
lieve to - day, For in the prom-ise all may share, To
Christ the Son, This "who-so-ev - er" is for thee, To

Chorus.

"who - so - ev - er" we pro-claim. ⎫
"who - so - ev - er" we re - peat. ⎪ And the Spirit and the bride say
"who - so - ev - er" we de - clare. ⎬
"who - so - ev - er" thou may be. ⎭

come, ... And let him that heareth say come, ... And let
come, come, come,   come, come, come,

him that is a-thirst come, ... And who-so-ev - er will, let him
let him come,

take the wa-ter of life free- ly, And who- so-ev - er will,. .. ...
let him come,

And who - so-ev - er will,.......... And who - so - ev - er
let him come,

will,............ Let him take the wa-ter of life free - ly.
let him come, And

GLORIOUS THINGS OF THEE.

D. B. TOWNER.

1. Glo-rious things of thee are spok-en, Zi - on, cit - y of our
2. Sav - ior, if in Zi - on's cit - y, I thro' grace a mem - ber

God; He, whose word cannot be broken, Form'd thee for His own abode.
am, Let the world deride or pit - y, I will glo-ry in Thy love.

CHORUS.

On the Rock of A - ges found - ed,

On the Rock...... : of A - ges found - ed, What can

What can shake thy sure re - pose? With sal-va-tion's walls sur-

shake......thy sure re - pose? With sal-va - - tion's walls surround-ed, Thou canst smile at all thy foes. With sal-

rounded, Thou canst smile...... at all thy foes.

vation's walls sur-round-ed, Thou canst smile at all thy foes.

WONDERFUL PEACE.

Rev. W. D. CORNELL, alt.   Rev. W. G. COOPER. Arr.

1. Far a-way in the depths of my spir-it to-night, Rolls a
2. What a treas-ure I have in this won-der-ful peace, Bur-ied
3. I am rest-ing to-night in this won-der-ful peace, Rest-ing
4. And methinks when I rise to that cit-y of peace, Where the
5. Ah! soul, are you here without comfort or rest, Marching

mel - o - dy sweeter than psalm; In ce-les - tial-like strains it un-
deep in the heart of my soul; So se-cure that no pow-er can
sweet-ly in Je - sus' con - trol; For I'm kept from all danger by
au - thor of peace I shall see, That one strain of the song which the
down the rough pathway of time? Make Je-sus your friend ere the

Copyright, 1894, by D. B. Towner.

ceas - ing - ly falls O'er my soul like an in - fi - nite calm.
mine it a - way, While the years of e - ter - ni - ty roll.
night and by day, And His glo - ry is flood-ing my soul.
ran-somed shall sing In that heav-en - ly king-dom will be.
shad - ows grow dark, Oh, ac - cept of this peace so sub - lime.

CHORUS.

Peace! peace! won - der - ful peace, Com - ing down from the

Fa - ther a bove; Sweep o - ver my spir - it for-

ev - er I pray In fa - thom-less bil-lows of love.

HORATIUS BONAR **D b TOWNER**

1. O Light of light shine in! Cast out this night of sin.
2. O Joy of joys come in! End Thou this grief of sin,
3. O Life of life pour in! Ex - pel this death of sin,
4. O Love of love flow in! This hate - ful root of sin
5. My God and Lord, oh, come! Of joys the Joy and sum.

Cre - ate true day with - in; O Light of light shine in.
Cre - ate calm peace with - in; O Joy of joys come in.
A - wake true life with - in; O Life of life pour in.
Pluck up, de - stroy with - in; O Love of love flow in.
Make in this heart Thy home; My God and Lord, oh, come.

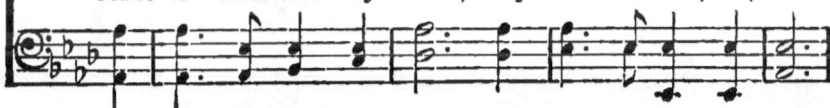

Shine in,...... O Light shine in! Cast out.....this night of sin;
Shine. in, Cast out

Cre - ate true day with - in; O Light of light shine in.

SOME SWEET DAY.

A. W. FRENCH.

D. B. TOWNER.

1. We shall reach the riv-er side, Some sweet day, some sweet day;
2. We shall pass in-side the gate, Some sweet day, some sweet day;
3. We shall meet our loved and own, Some sweet day, some sweet day;

We shall cross the storm-y tide, Some sweet day, some sweet day;
Peace and plen-ty for us wait, Some sweet day, some sweet day;
Gath'ring round the great white throne, Some sweet day, some sweet day;

We shall press the sands of gold, While be-fore our eyes un-fold
We shall hear the wond'rous strain, Glo-ry to the Lamb that's slain,
By the tree of life so fair, Joy and rap-ture ev-'ry-where,

Heav-en's splendors, yet un-told, Some sweet day, some sweet day.
Christ was dead, but lives again, Some sweet day, some sweet day.
Oh, the bliss of o-ver there! Some sweet day, some sweet day.

I SHALL BE SATISFIED.

35

Arr. by Rev G W. Crofts.   By per of T C O'Kane.   Arr by D B. T.

1. When I shall wake in that fair morn of morns, Aft-er whose dawning
2. When I shall meet the dear ones I have loved, Who once a-long my
3. When I shall meet my Shepherd and His fold, And taste a-new the
4. When I in heav'n shall "know as I am known," And there from Christ shall

night no more re-turns, And in whose glo-ry day e-ter-nal burns,
path-way sweetly moved, And see how faith-ful God to me has proved,
love of Christ un-told, And walk for aye the shin-ing streets of gold,
take my robe and crown, And reap in joy what I in tears have sown,

REFRAIN.

I shall be sat-is-fied.   I shall be sat-is-fied,

I shall be sat-is-fied,   I shall be sat-is-fied, oye and bye.

Copyright, 1893, by D. B. Towner.

MAN THE LIFE-BOAT.

JOHN R. CLEMENTS.   D. B. TOWNER.

1. Man the life-boat! quick, my broth-er, Send it speed-ing
2. Man the life-boat! to the res-cue! Hast-en, hast-en
3. Man the life-boat! strug-gling sea-men! Bat-tle now with
4. Man the life-boat! God will aid you; Out a-cross life's

o'er the wave, If you hast-en to the res-cue, Some poor
on your way! With the bea-con lights to guide you, From the
rag-ing wave! See! they cling to spar and tim-ber, Pre-cious
storm-tossed wave, Wrecks the wa-ters dark are strew-ing, On them

sail-or you may save, Sink-ing fast in sin's dark wa-ters,
wreck you can-not stray; Speed a-way, the ship is sink-ing,
lives your hand can save; Leaps the an-gry surge a-bout them
some whom you can save; Car-ry quick the cups of com-fort,

Help-less 'mid the break-ers high, Man the life-boat! quick, oh,
Go and work 'mid scenes of woe; Man the life-boat! nerve for
As to drown their plead-ing cry, Man the life-boat! flash your
Pick them up in Je-sus' name, Man the life-boat! res-cue

hast - en, To the res - cue, ere they die.
ac - tion, To the res - cue, broth-er, go.
sig - nal! Let them know that help is nigh.
some one, From the wreck some soul reclaim.

CHORUS.

A-way! a - way! God's

Spir - it speed you, Res-cue some poor soul to - day! A - way, a-way!

God's Spir - it lead you, To the res - cue, speed a - way.

SOWING AND REAPING.

JOSEPHINE POLLARD.　　　　　E A PERKINS. Arr.

1. Out on the highways, wher-ev-er we go, Seed we must gath-er and
2. Here, where it seems but a wilderness place, Wanting in beau-ty and
3. Out of those gardens so gorgeous with flow'rs, Seed we may gather to
4. Out of each moment some good we ob-tain, Something to winnow and
5. That which we gather is that which we sow, Seed-time and harvest al-

Copyright, 1893. by D. B. Towner.

seed we must sow;　E - ven the tin - i - est　seed has a pow'r,
want-ing in grace, Some lit - tle crea-ture in ten - der - ness goes,
beau - ti - fy　ours, While from our own lit - tle　plot we may share,
scat - ter a - gain,　All that we lis - ten to, all that we　read,
ter - nate-ly　flow, When we have finished with time, 'twill be known

CHORUS.

Be　it　of this - tle　or　be　it of flow'r. Gath　-　er - ing
Plucking the net - tle　and planting the rose.
Something to ren-der　our neigh-bor's more fair.
All that we think of,　is gath - er - ing seed.
How we have gathered and how we have sown. Gathering seed we must

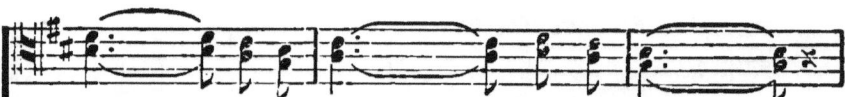

seed ..... we must scat　-　-　ter as well,........
scatter as well,　　Gath - er-ing seed we must scatter as well,

God ..... will watch o　-　ver the place...... where it
God will watch over the place where it fell,　God will watch o-ver the

fell,......... On - ly the gain.. of the har - vest is
place where it fell, On - ly the gain of the har - vest is

ours,.. Shall we plant net-tles, or shall we plant flow'rs?

THEY WALKED AND TALKED WITH JESUS.

M. D. JAMES.   From KUCKEN, Arr. by D. B. T.

1. They walked and talked with Je - sus And knew not it was He, Who
2. And then, unveiled before them, The Sav - ior stood revealed; The
3. And with His dear dis - ci - ples, He walks and talks to-day, "Lo!

gave His life a   ran - som To set the cap-tive free;   His
bless-èd ris - en   Je - sus, No long-er was concealed;   Oh,
I am with you   al - ways," We hear Him gen - tly say;   Oh,

words of ho - ly pow - er,   His look of match-less grace, Seemed
won-drous rev - e - la - tion, The God and Man com-bined! The
bliss - ful hour, when Je-sus Un - veils His glo-ri - ous face, And

more than those of   mor - tal, And charmed their wond'ring gaze.
great I Am— Al - might-y— In hu - man flesh en-shrined.
shows His sav - ing pow - er, And His a - maz-ing grace.

CHORUS.

Oh, to thus commune with Thee! All the jour-ney, liv-ing,

dy - ing,—Oh, to walk and talk with Thee! 'Tis heav'n begun below.

I NEED THEE, PRECIOUS JESUS. 41

Rev. F. Whitfield. J. D. F. Arr. by D. B. Towner.

1. I need Thee, pre-cious Je-sus! For I am full of
2. I need Thee, pre-cious Je-sus! I need a friend like
3. I need Thee, pre-cious Je-sus! I need Thee ev-'ry
4. I need Thee, pre-cious Je-sus! And hope to see Thee

sin,.. My soul is dark and guilt-y, My heart is dead with-
Thee, A friend to soothe and com-fort, A friend to care for
day, To fill me with Thy full-ness, To lead me on my
soon, En-cir-cled with the rain-bow, And seat-ed on Thy

in; I need the cleans-ing fount-ain, Where I can al-ways
me; I need the heart of Je-sus, To feel each anx-ious
way; I need Thy ho-ly Spir-it To teach me who I
throne; There with Thy blood-bought peo-ple, My joy shall ev-er

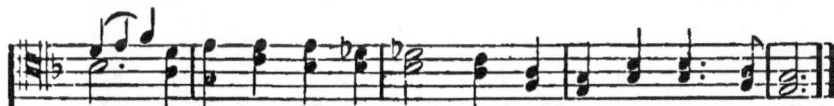

flee; The blood of Christ most precious, The sin-ner's on-ly plea.
care, To bear my ev-'ry bur-den, And all my sor-rows share.
am, To show me more of Je-sus, To point me to the Lamb;
be, To praise Thee, precious Je-sus, To gaze, my Lord, on Thee.

JESUS IS KNOCKING.

T. B. A.   T. B. ATKINSON.

1. The Sav-ior has come to a - bide with thee, Wea - ry one,
2. The Sav-ior a feast has pre-pared for thee, Hun - gry one,
3. A sur-cease from sor-row the Sav - ior brings, Glad - less one,
4. The Sav-ior may turn from thy door a - way, Care - less one,

worn by sin; He stand-eth out-side of thy bolt - ed door,
starved by sin; Then o - pen the door of thy heart just now,
bowed by sin; Re - sist not His ef - fort to suc - cor thee,
court - ing sin; If long - er you lin - ger with Sa - tan's throng,

CHORUS.

Oh, o - pen and let Him in.   List-en, knocking,
And let the dear Sav - ior in.
But hast-en and let Him in.
A-rouse, then, and let Him in.   List-en, knocking,

1. Jesus is knocking, oh, bid Him come in;   2. Bid the dear Savior come in.

HE SLUMBERS NOT.

CLARA L. SHATTUCK.

D. B. TOWNER.

43

1. Fret not thy-self, my heart! The Lord hath care for thee; Tho'
2. He com - pass - es thy path, And know-eth all thy ways; A
3. To Him a thou - sand years Are but as yes - ter - day; An
4. Be si - lent, O my soul! Let thy com-plain - ing cease; On

des - o - late and poor thou art, He shall thy por - tion be;
pur - pose true of love He hath, Which runs throughout thy days;
hour, an age, the same ap-pears— He chang-eth not for aye;
Him thy bur-den thou may'st roll, And walk henceforth in peace;

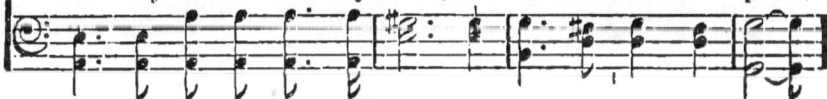

His cov - e - nant........stands firm and sure,........ His mer-cy
He sees the end ..... thou canst not see,....... . And what He
And soon or late,........ in shade or sun, ... His plan is
Where He a - bides........ all storms are stilled,...... And ev - 'ry

His cov - e-nant stands firm and sure,

CHORUS.

ev - - - er shall en - dure. He slumbers not,..........
wills 1........ is best for thee.
wrought,..... His will is done.
need........ is more than filled. He slumbers not,

His mer-cy ev er shall en - dure.

He will not sleep,........ All safe thou art,........ for He doth
He will not sleep,   All safe thou art,

keep, (doth keep,) Hold firm thy trust, ... tho' clouds a -
for He doth keep,   Hold firm thy trust,

rise........ In God's good hand.... thy fu-ture lies,........
tho' clouds arise,   In God's good hand thy fu-ture lies, (thy future lies.)

YE MUST BE BORN AGAIN.

Rev. W. T. SLEEPER.   GEO. C. STEBBINS.

1. A ru-ler once came un-to Je-sus by night, To
2. Ye chil-dren of men, now at-tend to the word, So
3. Oh, ye who would en-ter that glo-ri-ous rest, And
4. A dear one in heav-en thy heart yearns to see, And

ask Him the way to sal - va - tion and light, The Master made
sol - emn - ly ut-tered by Je - sus, the Lord, And let not the
sing with the ransomed the song of the blest, The life ev - er -
now at the gate, may be wait ing for thee, Then list to the

an-swer in words true and plain, "Ye must be born a - gain"...
mes-sage to you be in vain "Ye must be born a - gain"....
last - ing if ye would ob - tain, "Ye must be born a - gain"....
note of this sol - emn re - frain, "Ye must be born a - gain"....
again.

CHORUS.

"Ye must be born a - gain,.... Ye must be born a - gain,.. I
again, again.

ver-i- ly, ver-i-ly say un-to thee, Ye must be born again."(a-gain.)

LISTEN TO HIS VOICE.

Ella Lauder.

D. B. Towner.

1. Hark! a gen - tle whis-per, on - ly thou canst hear,
2. Je - sus stand - eth knock - ing at thy heart's closed door,
3. If you do not list - en He will turn a - way,

Tell - ing thee, oh, sin - ner, that the Lord is near;
Bring-ing thee a bless - ing from His bounteous store;
Heed the lov - ing mes - sage, wan - d'rer, while you may,

Do not drown His plead-ings by the gay world's din,
Wait-ing to be gra - cious to thy need - y soul,
Lest when you shall o - pen wide the fast - barred door,

List - en as He bids thee turn a - way from sin.
By His grace to heal thee, if thou wilt be whole.
Je - sus shall be wait - ing there for thee no more.

List-en, list-en, list-en to His voice, Call-ing, call-ing, bid-ding you re-joice, 'Tis thy Sav-ior call-ing, come, oh, come to Me, Haste! He will not al-ways call and wait for thee.

THE SURE REFUGE.

F. S. SHEPHARD.   D. B. TOWNER.

1. Loud-ly roar the storms of sin, Fierce without and fierce within;
2. Strong tempt-a-tions now assail, What a-gainst them can a-vail?
3. Now a-bove the foe a-rise, Seek to gain "th' immortal prize;"

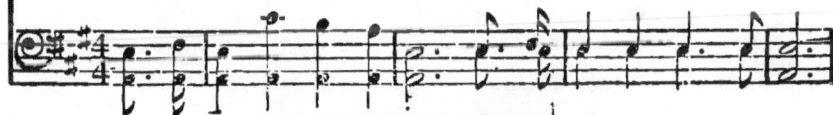

He a-lone can vic-t'ry win, Whose feet are on "The Rock."
He a-lone will sure pre-vail, Whose feet are on "The Rock."
Pow'rs of e-vil he de-fies, Whose feet are on "The Rock."

CHORUS.

"Rock of A ges," ref-uge sure, That for-
"Rock of A-ges," ref-uge sure,

ev er will en-dure, Mid the storms...... it
That for-ev-er will en-dure, Mid the storms

stands se-cure, "Rock of A ges," refuge sure, refuge sure.
it stands secure, "Rock of Ages," ref-uge sure, refuge sure.

THE EVERLASTING ARMS.

49

IDA L. REED.

WM. J. KIRKPATRICK.

1. There's a tho't that cheers me ev - er, Keeps my soul from all a-
2. Tho' the skies are dark a - bove me, Thorn - y be the path be-
3. What tho' griefs and care en- cum - ber, Wea - ry bur - dens press me
4. Oh, the peace the sweet hope bringeth, And my soul is sat - is-

larms, I shall find e - ter-nal ref- uge In the Ev - er -lasting Arms.
low, He will safely keep who loves me, And my soul no fear shall know.
long, When His kindness I remem-ber, This shall ev-er be my song.
fied, And my heart within me singeth I shall safely there a-bide.

REFRAIN.

In the Ev - er - last-ing Arms, In the Ev - er - last-ing Arms,

We shall find e - ter-nal ref-uge In the Ev - er-last - ing Arms.

AT THY FEET.

Words arranged.

T. H. Atkinson.

1. At Thy feet, O bless-.ed Je - sus, Let me learn of Thee!
2. Learn the cost of my re-demp - tion, Learn Thy pow'r to save;
3. Learn to heed Thy gen-tle prompt-ings, Learn to know Thy voice;
4. Learn to know Thee yet more whol - ly, Learn Thy per-fect will;
5. Learn to list-en for the com - ing Of Thy bless-ed feet;

Lay - ing down each heav-y bur - den, From all care set free;
Learn of that bright res - ur-rec - tion From the aw - ful grave;
Learn to bear my dai - ly bur - den, Learn to still re - joice;
If that will is not re - veal - ed, Learn to wait there still;
Learn to find my chief-est pleas - ure In com - mun - ion sweet;

Hal - lowed is mine in - ner cham - ber, Bide Thou here with me!
Learn how boundless is Thy mer - cy, That un - ceas - ing flows;
Learn to be more pa-tient, ho - ly, Seek-ing not my own;
Learn the se - cret of Thy pow - er O - ver hearts of men;
Hal - lowed is my in - ner cham - ber Bide Thou here with me!

At Thy feet a lit - tle sea - son, Let me learn of Thee!
Learn to prize and keep the glo - ry That Thy love be - stows;
Learn that hu - man arms must fail me, Lean on Thee a - lone.
Learn Thou hast my sins for-giv - en, Learn it o'er a - gain.
At Thy feet, O Je - sus, Mas - ter, Let me learn of Thee.

Copyright, 1893, by D. B. Towner.

A. S. K.

A. S. KIEFFER.

1. Come to our Fa - ther's house, Come ere the day is gone;
2. Look at the wea - ry way, Look where thy feet have trod;
3. Dark - er thy path-way grows, Soon will the night come down;
4. Fly from the fields of sin, Fly for thy life to - day;
5. Here will thy soul find rest, Safe from each an - gry blast;

Tem-pests are gath'ring fast, Dark-ness is com ing on.
Find-ing no rest, no peace, Wan-d'ring a-way from God.
Fierce-ly the lightnings flash, Dark - er the tem pests frown.
Fly to our Fa - ther's house, En - ter the nar row way.
Here find a per - fect peace, Joys that for - ev er last.

CHORUS.

Fly, for the tempest is com-ing, Sweeping the fields of sin;

Knock at the por-tals of mer cy, Je - sus will let you in.

By permission.

I SING.

F. S. S.

F. S. SHEPHARD. Arr.

1. I sing, for my Savior and King Has giv'n me peace for my woe;
2. I sing, for my Savior and King Has taken my heart for His throne,
3. I sing, for my Savior and King Has chosen my la-bors to bless,
4. I sing, for my Savior and King Is com-ing a-gain for His own,

And now that I've tested His love, I'll praise Him wherever I go.
And what can I do but re-joice, He calls me His loved and His own.
And, as I go forth in His name, My pleasure I can but ex-press.
We'll meet Him, and reign with Him there, Joint-heirs to His king-dom and throne.

CHORUS.

I sing! I sing! The prais-es of Je-sus I sing!
I sing! I sing! I sing!

I sing! I sing! Of Je-sus, my Savior and King!
I sing! I sing! my King!

WHAT MORE COULD HE DO?

Rev. J. H. Sammis.   D. B. Towner.

1. Oh, won-der-ful, won-der-ful grace! Oh, sto-ry so
2. For sin, oh, how dear-ly He paid, Your soul to re-
3. What more could He suf-fer to pay The debt un-to
4. What more could He suf-fer to prove The love of the

sweet and so true, Of Je-sus who died in our place! What
deem from its woe! A full sat-is-fac-tion He made, Oh,
right-eous-ness due? For mer-cy to o-pen the way, My
Fa-ther for you? Thy heart with con-tri-tion to move, Say

CHORUS.

more, oh, what more could He do?
broth-er, what more could He do?   } What more could He do, what
broth-er, what more could He do?
broth-er, what more could He do?

more could He do? Say, brother, what more could He do? He shed His own

Copyright, 1893, by D. B. Towner.

blood for a sin-cleans-ing flood, Oh, brother, what more could He do?

REMEMBER ME, O MIGHTY ONE.

Anon.   JOANNA KINKEL.

1. When storms around are sweeping, When lone my watch I'm keeping,
2. When walk-ing on life's o-cean, Con-trol its rag-ing mo-tion;
3. When weight of sin op-press-es, When dark de-spair dis-tress-es,

Mid fires of e-vil fall-ing, Mid tempters' voic-es call-ing,
When from its dangers shrinking, When in its dread deeps sinking,
All thro' the life that's mor-tal, And when I pass death's portal,

Remember me, O Mighty One! Remember me, O Mighty One!

Mrs. A. L. Davidson.   J. H. Fillmore.

1. O'er heav'nly plains the golden chimes Of Zi-on ring to-day;   For
2. And we, who walk in earth-ly vales, Their joy-ful music hear, In
3. They call us home, not here our rest, They softly seem to say: Be-

REFRAIN.

passing souls those chimes are rung, To guide them on their way. Sweet bells,......
mel-o-dy di-vine-ly sweet, So faint and yet so clear.
yond the gates of Zion fair There shines a brighter day. Sweet chiming Zion

.... sweet bells,......... sweet bells, They cheer us on our pleasant way, Sweet
bells, Sweet chiming Zion bells,   They cheer our way,   Sweet

chiming bells, They cheer us on our pleasant way, Sweet chiming bells.
They cheer our way,....

DEAR SAVIOR, COME IN.

C. L. SHACKLOCK.   D. B. TOWNER.

The verses should be sung as a Duet. 1st & 2d Tenor.

1. I'm a-thirst for the fount-ain of mer-cy, My soul is o'er-
2. I have wandered so long in the dark-ness, So far from the
3. Let the light of Thy presence for-ev-er Il-lu-mine the

burdened with sin, And the tears of re-pent-ance are fall-ing,
path of the blest, I am wea-ry, and faint, and I'm sigh-ing
depths of my heart, Thou art wait-ing e'en now on the threshold,

CHORUS.

Come in, bless-ed Sav-ior, come in. Come in, come in, My
For pit-y, for par-don and rest.
Oh, en-ter, no more to de-part. Come in, come in,

soul is so wea-ry of sin; .... The door of my
Come in, for

heart is now o - pen, Come in, dear Sav - ior, come in.

O SILVERY SEA OF GALILEE.

Fronia Smith.   Fred. A. Fillmore.

1. O silv'ry sea...... of Gali-lee,   In eastern land so fair;
2. I hear the cry,.. "Save, Lord, I pray,"From one, faint-hearted, there;
3. The night is dark,.. I'm on a sea   Where waves roll high and wild;

1. O silv'ry sea   of Galilee, In east-ern land so fair;

In fan-cy   now........ I stand by thee,   And
My sinking heart........ takes up that cry,   When
I'm lost un-less...... . Thou pi-lot   me,   O

In fan-cy now   I stand by thee, And

see   my Sav-ior there; I see Him walk.......... up-on the
storms beat heav-y here: For well I   know.......... His gracious
Mas - ter, strong and mild; Walk to me on............ this troubled

see   my Sav-ior there;   I see Him walk

O SILVERY SEA OF GALILEE.

wave,.... When billows roll...... and clouds are dark:.. His trembling
will...... Can calm life's rough... and troubled sea: ....And to its
sea,...... Dear Savior, bid....... me walk to Thee..... I shall not

upon the wave,   When billows roll   and clouds are dark;

ones. ...from death to save,   Tossed helpless in their bark.
waves .... say. "Peace, be still,"   As there on Gal-i - lee.
fail....... for Thou wilt save.   As once on Gal-i - lee.

His trembling ones   from death to save, Tossed helpless in their bark.

RIDE ON, O LORD.

Words altered.   D. B. TOWNER.

1. Now be the gos-pel ban - ner   In ev - 'ry land unfurled,
2. Yes, Thou shalt reign for - ev - er,   O Je - sus, King of kings!

And be the shout Ho-san - na!   Re - ech-oed thro' the world: Till
Thy light. Thy love, Thy fa - vor.   Each ransomed captive sings: The

ev - 'ry isle and na - tion, Till ev - 'ry tribe and tongue,
isles for Thee are wait - ing, The des - erts learn Thy praise;

Re - ceive the great sal - va - tion, And join the hap-py throng.
The hills and val-leys greet-ing, The song re - spons-ive raise.

CHORUS.

Ride on, O Lord, vic-to - ri-ous, Immanuel, Prince of Peace;
Ride on, O Lord, vic-to - ri-ous, Im-man - uel, Prince of Peace;

Thy triumph shall be glo - ri-ous, Thy empire still increase.
Thy tri - umph shall be glo - ri-ous, Thy em - pire still increase.

60

DRIFTING.

E. E. HEWITT.   WM. J. KIRKPATRICK.

1. Where-fore art thou wrapt in slum - ber? Drift - ing on
2. Drift - ing while the sky is sun - ny; Balm - y per-
3. Rouse thee, rouse thee from thy dream-ing! Sleep - er on
4. I - dly drift - ing then no long - er, Sav - ing oth-

so aim - less - ly; Know thou not time's fit - ful wa - ters
fume fills the air, Charm - ing thee to fa - tal slum - ber,
a treach'rous tide; Help - less on a sea of per - il,
ers out at sea; Speed - ing on - ward to His glo - ry,

REFRAIN.

Hast-en towards E-ter-ni-ty? Drifting, drifting, drifting, drifting,
Not a tho't and not a pray'r. Drifting, drifting, drifting, drifting,
Call the Savior to thy side. Drifting, drifting, drifting, drifting,
Towards a bright E-ter-ni - ty. Speeding, speeding, speeding, speeding,

To the great E - ter-ni - ty, To the great E - ter-ni - ty.

Copyright, 1893, by Wm. J. Kirkpatrick.

WE'LL NEVER SAY GOOD-BY.

Mrs. E. W. Chapman.   J. H. Tenney.

1. Our friends on earth we meet with pleasure, While swift the moments fly,
2. How joy-ful is the tho't that lingers, When loved ones cross death's sea;
3. No part-ing words shall e'er be spoken In that bright land of flow'rs,

Yet ev - er comes the tho't of sad-ness That we must say good-by.
That when our la-bors here are end - ed, With them we'll ever be.
But songs of joy, and peace, and gladness, Shall ev - er-more be ours.

Chorus.

We'll never say good-by in heav'n, We'll never say good-by (good-by),

Repeat Chorus pp.

For in that land of joy and song, We'll never say good- by.

ALTOGETHER LOVELY.

H. E. Jones.   D. B. Towner.

UNISON OR SOLO.   ALL PARTS.

1. The One who suffered on the tree, Is the Chief a-mong ten thousand;
2. The One who guards each step I take—Is the Chief a-mong ten thousand:
3. Oh, yes, my Je-sus is the Chief—Is the Chief a-mong ten thousand;

UNISON OR SOLO.   ALL PARTS.

The One who gave His life for me,—Is the Chief a-mong ten
The One who nev-er will for-sake—Is the Chief a-mong ten
The One so near in joy or grief—Is the Chief a-mong ten

DUET.

thousand: The One who died the world to save, Who rose in triumph
thousand; The One who helps me day by day, Who meets me when I
thousand; The One who sweet-ly saves the soul. Who in the heart holds

ALL PARTS.

from the grave, That all e-ter-nal life may have—Is the Chief among ten
kneel to pray, Who leads me all along the way—Is the Chief among ten
glad con-trol, Whose reign shall last while ages roll—Is the Chief among ten

ALTOGETHER LOVELY.

CHORUS.

thou-sand. Oh, yes,.... He is the Chief: Is the
thou-sand. Oh, yes, He is the Chief, is the Chief, Is the

Chief a - mong ten thou - sand; Oh, yes,..... He is the
Chief a - mong ten thou - sand; Oh, yes, He is the

One That is al - to - geth - er love - ly.
One, is the One That is al - to - geth - er love - ly.

DON'T KEEP JESUS WAITING.

Rev. G. W. CROFTS.   C. C. CLINE.

1. Don't keep Je - sus wait - ing, Wait - ing ev - er - more;
2. Don't keep Je - sus wait - ing, Wait - ing at the door;
3. Don't keep Je - sus wait - ing, Friend He is, and more;
4. Don't keep Je - sus wait - ing, Till the day is o'er;

By permission.

DON'T KEEP JESUS WAITING.

Hark! He knocketh soft - ly   At   thy   bo - som's   door;
How He suf - fered for   Thee;   All   thy   sins He   bore;
As   thy Sav - ior loves thee,   None e'er   loved be - fore;
Sad should Je - sus leave thee,   Leave thee   ev - er - more;

I............. im - plore.

Haste that door to   o - pen,   O - pen, I   im - plore.
Bid Him free - ly   en - ter,   Bid Him, I   im - plore.
Do   not turn Him from thee,   Do not, I   im - plore.
Wide the   door fling o - pen,   O - pen, I   im - plore.

I............. im - plore.

SWEETLY O'ER MY SOUL.

T. H. A.   THOS. H. ATKINSON.

1. Sweet - ly   o'er my soul now stealing, Comes the Spirit of my Lord,
2. Bliss - ful   are my qui - et slumbers, Fanned by Canaan's perfumed breeze;
3. Wake me not from my rev - er - ie, On the bo - som of my Lord,

Calming all   the troubled wa - ters, Har - mo - niz - ing each dis - cord.
Lost to con - sciousness of heart-ache, Soothed by heav'nly melodies.
Earth no more can soothe or charm me, Let me bide with heav'n's adored.

HELP ME TO BE HOLY.

A. J. GORDON. D. D.

D. B. TOWNER.

1. Help me to be ho - ly, O Fa - ther of light;
2. Help me to be ho - ly, O Sav - ior di - vine;
3. Help me to be ho - ly, O Spir - it di - vine;

Guilt-burdened and low - ly, I bow in Thy sight;
Why con-quer so slow - ly This na-ture of mine?
Come, sanc-ti - fy whol - ly This tem-ple of Thine;

How shall a stained con-science Dare gaze on Thy face;
Stamp deep-ly Thy like - ness Where Sa-tan's hath been;
Now cast out each i - dol, Here set up Thy throne;

E'en though in Thy pres - ence Thou graut me a place?
Sub - due with Thy bright - ness My dark-ness and sin.
Reign, reign, without ri - val, Su - preme and a - lone.

HE LEADETH ME.

J. H. ROSECRANS.

Moderato. *p*   *p*

He leadeth me,   He leadeth me,
He holdeth me,   He holdeth me,
1. He lead-eth me,   He lead-eth me,   Although I cannot
2. He hold-eth me,   He hold-eth me,   Because I cannot

3. He comforts me,   He comforts me,   He speaks so tender-
4. He lov-eth me,   He lov-eth me,   Ah! well I know that
He comforts me,   He comforts me,
He lov-eth me,   He lov-eth me,

see One step be-fore my face; The way I can-not trace; My
be Left to my failing strength, For I should fall at length; I

ly To cheer me on my way; And al-ways bids me lay My
He, My best, most loving Friend, Will lead me to the end; I

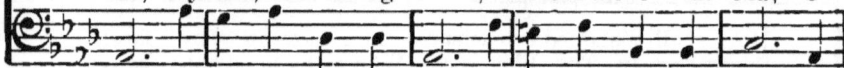

rit. e dim.

sight is dim, and so, He lead-eth me,   He lead-eth me.
am so weak, and so, He hold-eth me,   He hold-eth me.
He leadeth me,
He holdeth me,

cares on Him, and thus He com-forts me,   He comforts me.
love Him, too, because He lov-eth me,   He lov-eth me.
He comforts me,
He lov-eth me,

I AM THY CHILD.

ANDREW SHERWOOD.　　　　　　　　　　　D. B. TOWNER.

1. Fa - ther, when bil - lows round me roll, And waves are
2. Fa - ther, when tem-pests o - ver - whelm, And night o'er-
3. Fa - ther, when winds and waves sub - side, And storms are
4. Fa - ther, the voy - age soon will cease; On shores where

like the mount-ains piled, One bless-ed thought with rap-ture fills my
takes me, dark and wild; I'll fear no ill for Thou dost hold the
hushed to zeph-yrs mild; O'er sap-phire seas I'll safe - ly homeward
end - less morn hath smiled, I'll anch - or safe with-in the port of

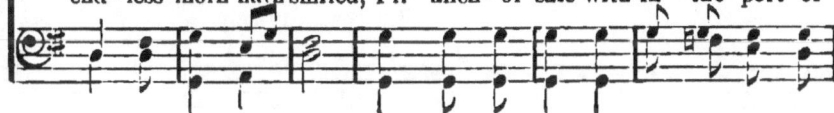

CHORUS.

soul— I am Thy child.
helm—I am Thy child. } Oh, bliss-ful, blissful tho't, Oh, tho't with-
glide—I am Thy child. {
peace—I am Thy child.

out al - loy, My soul doth shout for joy,—I am Thy child.

ABIDE IN ME.

Joseph R. Wheeler.   J. H. Rosecrans.

1. A-bide in me; tread not the thorny path a - lone
2. A-bide in me dear one; the way I've trod be-fore

1. A-bide in me;..........
2. A-bide in me.........

The way is dark and drear,   Put thou thy trust in
I know its pierc-ing thorns,   Put thou thy help-less
                            Put thou thy trust,.......... in
                            Put thou thy help . . . - less

me, I'll lead thee safe-ly on, Dis - pel thy doubts and fear;
hand in mine, and fear no more, And safe I'll lead thee on;

For this I came from mine own Father's throne,   To lead His children
A-bide in me as branch doth in the vine,   Around me fast thy
                    For this I came from mine own Father's throne,
                    Abide in me as branch doth in the viue,

Copyright, 1894, by D. B. Towner.

thro' the darkness lone,   And give them peace along their
feeble arms entwine,   And   I will keep thee ev-e-
To lead His children thro' the darkness lone,
Around me fast thy feeble arms entwine,

Rit. e dim.

journey home: Fear not, abide in me........
more as Mine   Doubt not, a-bide in me........
And give them peace along their journey home: Fear not, abide in me.
And I will keep thee evermore as Mine.   Doubt not, abide in me.

SOMEWHERE TO-NIGHT.

Rev R. M. OFFORD.   D. B. TOWNER.
DUET. 1st Tenor & 1st Bass.

1. A moth-er dear is weep-ing, Some-where to-night,
2. A moth-er's low-ly bend-ing, Some-where to-night,
3. A moth-er's heart is break-ing, Some-where to-night,
4. A moth-er still is plead-ing, Some-where to-night,

Some-where to-night, Ma-ny and bit-ter the tears she weeps,
Some-where to-night, Bow-ing and pleading with God in pray'r,
Some-where to-night, Breaking with sor-row, with shame and grief
Some-where to-night, Plead-ing, still plead-ing for one a-stray.

Wea - ry the vig - il and sad she keeps, For, oh, she grieveth by
Bring-ing to Je - sus her load of care, She prays as moth-er a -
Where shall she find for her soul re-lief! A - las! for her there can
Mak - ing the prom-ise of God her stay, While faith and hope in her

night and day For one that wandereth far away From God and right.
lone can pray, For one that wandereth far away From God and right.
be no peace, Un-til her darling to wander cease From God and right.
bosom burn; Oh, come, thou wandering one, return To God and right.

CHORUS.

O wandering one,........ List, list to the plea; ....
    wandering one,   List to the plea;

Thy moth-er is pray-ing, is pray-ing for thee.

Andante. D. B. TOWNER.

1. Go   when the morning shin - eth,   Go when the noon   is bright;
2. Think then of all who love   Thee,   All who are loved by Thee:
3. Or,   if 'tis e'er de - nied thee   In   sol - i - tude to   pray:

Go when the eve de - clin - eth,   Go   in   the hush of night;
Pray, too, for those who hate   thee,   If   an - y   such there be;
Should ho - ly tho'ts come o'er   thee, When friends are round thy way;

Go with an hum-ble   feel - ing;   Put earth-ly thoughts a-way,
Then for thyself   in   meek - ness,   Hum-bly a bless-ing   claim,
E'en then the si - lent breath - ing   Thy spir - it lifts   a - bove,

And to the Mas-ter   kneel-ing,   Do   thou in se - cret pray.
Blending with each pe - ti - tion Thy great Redeemer's name.
Will reach His throne of glo - ry, Where dwells e - ter-nal   love.

SAVIOR, I COME TO THEE.

ANNIE D. BRADLEY.

J. H. ROSECRANS.

1. Sav-ior, lo!......... I come to Thee,.......... Trusting
2. Sav-ior, may...... my ev - 'ry thought........ Centered
3. Sav-ior, while...... on earth I live........... May I

1. Sav-ior, lo! I come to Thee,

to........... Thy gra - cious word,........ .... See! I
be........... up-on Thy love,............. And while
move........ at Thy com - mand,........... And may

Trusting to Thy gra - cious word,

cast......... my fears a - way,........... As I
Thou........ art guid-ing me,........... Al - so
I,.......... oh, lov - ing Lord,...... ..... Al-ways

See! I cast my fears a-way,

turn........ un-to my Lord!...........
teach........ me bow to serve;...........
clasp......... Thy help-ing hand,...........

As I turn un - to my Lord! Sav-ior,

SAVIOR, I COME TO THEE. 73

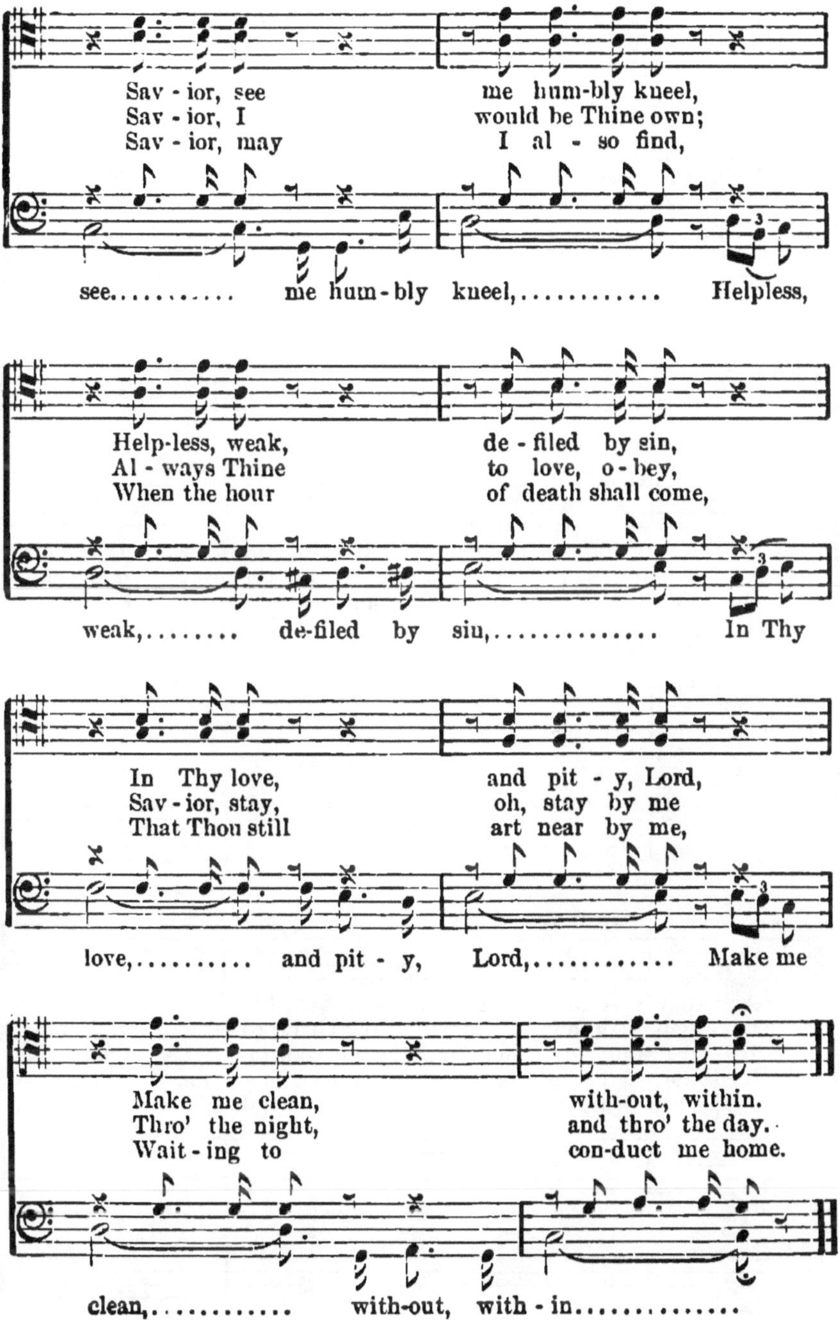

HE IS ABLE TO DELIVER.

MARY SPARKES WHEELER.
D. B. TOWNER.

1. When the prophet Dan - iel prayed to God on bend - ed knee,
2. Wherefore is the king so sad, and wherefore does he fast?
3. "O king, live for - ev - er!" and from anx-ious care be free,
4. From the roar-ing li - on, seek - ing whom he may de - vour,
5. He is a - ble to de - liv - er, and to keep in peace,

With his win-dows o - pen wide, despite the king's de - cree;
As he thinks of Dan-iel, who with - in the den is cast;
For my God has sent His an - gel to de - liv - er me;
God is a - ble to de - liv - er by His might - y pow'r;
Till life's pil-grim-age is end - ed, and my con - flicts cease;

And they cast him in the li - ons' den, his life to close,
O thou serv-ant of the liv - ing God, tell me, I pray,
He has shut the li-ons' mouths, my soul in tri - umph sings,
And the soul who comes to Je - sus with his sins op - pressed,
And when Death, the lat-est en - e - my, shall end the strife,

God was a - ble to de - liv - er him from all his foes.
From the li - ons' cru - el pow - er, can He save to - day?
Oh, what joy to trust for shel-ter un - der - neath His wings.
He is a - ble to de - liv - er, and to give him rest.
He is a - ble to de - liv - er, and to crown with life.

CHORUS.

For God's an - - gel is en-camp - ing   Round a -
For God's au-gel is encamping, is en-camp-ing

bout........ all them that fear   Him,   He is
Round a-bout them, round a-bout all them that fear Him,

a - - ble to de - liv - er   All who put their trust in Him.
He is a-ble, He is a - ble to deliver All who put their trust in Him.

WE SHALL MEET.

Mrs. L. M. B. Bateman.   J. H. Rosecrans.

Andante. p   m

1. Eyes that have gladdened the world with their light, Touched by the
2. Hands we have held in love's ten-der - est clasp, Fold - ed for
3. Feet we have welcomed at set-ting of sun, Come nev - er-
4. Lips we have touched with affection's fond kiss, Heart that has

death-blight are sealed from our sight, On - ly to look on life's
ev - er a - way from our grasp, On - ly to lift in life's
more from the day's la - bor done, Why should we weep since mid
throbbed with love's answering bliss, Why should we mourn that in

glo - ri-fied shore, Free from all griev-ing and tears ev - er-more.
glad - dest ac-cord, Reach-ing in glo - ry the hand of our Lord.
pleas-ures un - told, Hap - py they roam thro' the pathways of gold?
heaven's bright throng They can give voice to love's in - fi - nite song?

WE SHALL MEET.

We shall meet....... no more to sev - er, When the
We shall meet no more to sev-er,

toils...... of earth are o'er, We shall live...... and love for-
When the toils of earth are o'er, toils are o'er, We shall live

ev - er, O - ver on........ the oth - er shore,
and love for-ev-er, O-ver on the oth - er shore, oth-er shore.

SOME DAY, SOMETIME.

ELLA LAUDER.   D. B. TOWNER.

1. Some day, some - time, the boats-man gray, O'er death's dark
2. Some day, some - time, our eyes shall see The King in
3. Some day, some - time, our hearts shall know Sweet peace and
4. Some day, some - time, thro' streets of gold, Our feet shall

Copyright, 1894, by D. B. Towner.

riv - er, far a - way, Shall guide us in - to end - less day,
wondrous maj- es - ty, And from earth's bondage we'll be free,
rest from earthly woe, And we shall leave these scenes be - low,
walk mid joys un-told, And boundless love shall then en - fold,

Chorus.

Some day, some gold-en day. Some day, sometime, we soft-ly

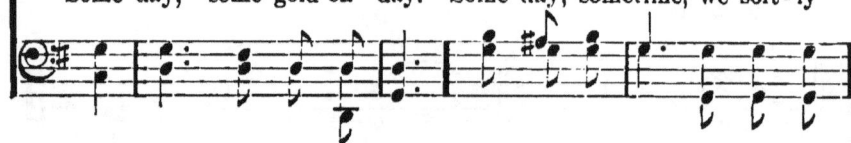

say, 'Twill sure - ly come, that glo - rious day, When Christ shall

Ritard.

call His own a - way, Some day, some gold - en day.

CAST THY BURDEN UPON THE LORD. 79

Rev. A. J. Gordon, D. D.   D. B. Towner.

1. Cast all thy care up - on the Lord, To Him for
2. Cast all thy sins up - on the Lord, He bore them
3. Cast all thy sor - rows on the Lord, Look up, the
4. Cast all thy bur - dens on the Lord, How-ev - er

suc - cor flee, Tho' high enthroned at God's right hand, He
on the tree, Be - hold, He liv - eth who was dead, And
nail - prints see! Thy name is gra - ven on His hands, He
great they be, Grief, pain and guilt, want, woe and fear, He

CHORUS.

care - eth still for thee. ⎫ Cast........ ...... thy bur - den up-
plead-eth still for thee. ⎪
suf - fers still with thee. ⎬ Cast thy burden upon the Lord,
bear - eth all for thee. ⎭

on............ the Lord, And He shall sus-
Cast thy bur-den up - on the Lord, And

CAST THY BURDEN UPON THE LORD.

tain thee, He shall sus - tain thee! Cast.......... thy
Cast thy bur-den up-

bur - - den up - on............ the Lord,........
on the Lord, Cast thy bur-den up - on the Lord.

Ritard.

And He shall sus-tain thee, He shall sus - tain thee.

I KNOW.

C. F. ATKINSON.

D. F. RANKIN.

1. E - ter - nal life is mine, I know, The bless - ed Je - sus
2. Not what I feel, or hope, or do, To heav'n can bring me
3. Oh, bless - ed joy I'm safe, I'm free, I stand in Christ's own
4. The pow'r of sin can - not pre-vail, Tho' all their darts my

tells me so, Up - on His pre-cious word I stand, And
safe - ly thro', My safe - ty lies in Christ a - lone, His
lib - er - ty, His blood has washed my crim - son stain, And
soul as - sail, For God's my Fa - ther, I'm His child, I

CHORUS.

naught can pluck me from His hand. ⎤
blood for me doth all a - tone. ⎥ For I know whom I
now I know I'm born a - gain. ⎥
know He'll guide me thro' the wild. ⎦

have be-lieved, I know His prom-ise ne'er deceived, What-

e'er my lot of earth-ly strife, I know I have e - ter-nal life.

82   I SING OF THE HOME-LAND.

ANDREW SHERWOOD.   D. B. TOWNER.

1. O'er all the hills of home-land, And thro' its peaceful vales,
2. My Sav-ior dwells in home-land, He's fair-est of the fair,
3. There is no death in home-land, No fun-'ral dirg-es toll,

The mu-sic of the ran-somed, Is float-ing on the
My friends who left me lone-ly, Are wait-ing for me
There is no sad, sad fare-well, No wea-ry, sin-sick

gales; A trav'ler to that country,—Our Father's fold a-bove, Here
there: A worn and weary trav'ler, I go to share their bliss, Far
soul; Christ bring us all to know Him, And save us by His truth, God

on the shores of earth-land, I sing of the home of love.
from my na-tive coun-try, I faint on the sands of this.
grant we find in home-land, The bloom of e-ter-nal youth.

CHORUS.

I sing of home and the home-land, Its joy and its beau-ty rare,

And smile to think of the greeting, That waits for me o - ver there.

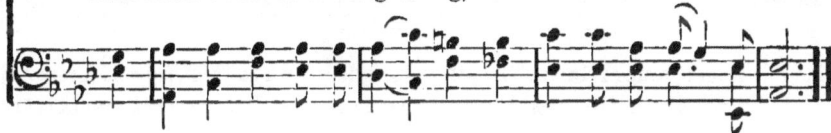

THE LOVE OF CHRIST.

D. B. TOWNER.

1. Love, love on earth appears, The wretched throng His way; He heareth all their
2. "I die for thee," He said, Be-hold the cross a - rise! And lo! He bows His
3. Now in the grave He's laid, In death's fu-ne-real gloom, Stern watchmen in the

Slow and soft.

griefs, And wipes their tears a-way; Soft and sweet the strain should be,
head, He bows His head and dies; Soft, my harp, thy breathings be,
shade, A seal up - on the tomb; Hushed, my harp, thy murmurs be,

pp   *Ritard.*

Sav - ior, when I sing to Thee, Sav-ior, when I sing to Thee.
Let me weep on Cal - va - ry, Let me weep on Cal - va - ry.
Christ is sleeping there for me, Christ is sleep-ing there for me.

f

4. The angel came at dawn, The stone is rolled a-way; The living dead is gone, And
5. He lives! again He lives! I hear the voice of love, He comes to soothe our fears And

bursts e - ter - nal day.   Loud and long the strain should be,
draw my soul a - bove.   Joy - ful now the strain should be,

ff

Jesus conquered death for me, Je-sus conquered death for me.
When I sing of Cal - va - ry, When I sing of Cal - va - ry.

IS IT SO?

Sarah Williams.

J. H. Rosecrans.

1. Is it so,.... O Christ in heaven, that the high-est suf-fer most,
2. Is it so,.... O Christ in heaven, that which-ever way we go,
3. Is it so,.... O Christ in heaven, that the full-ness yet to come,

That the strong - est wander farthest, and more hopelessly are lost,
Walls of dark - ness must surround us, things we would, but cannot know?
Is so glo - rious and so perfect that to know would strike us dumb?

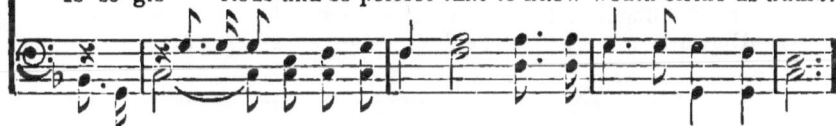

That the mark.... of rank in na - ture is ca-pac - i - ty for pain,
That the in - - fi-nite must bound us like a tem-ple veil un - rent,
That if on - - ly for a moment we would pierce beyond the sky,

That the an - - guish of the sing-er makes the sweetness of the strain?
While the fi - - nite ev - er wea-ries, so that none at-tains con-tent?
With these poor... dim eyes of mor-tals we should just see God and die?

I AM SAVED.

Andrew Sherwood.   D. B. Towner.

1. Would you know why I am glad? I am saved! I am
2. Let the storm and tem-pest come,—I am saved! I am
3. Sing my soul, and leap for joy, I am saved! I am
4. Oh! the blest as-sur-ance giv'n—I am saved! I am

saved! Sweetest joy man ev-er had, I am saved! I am
saved! I shall reach my heav'nly home, I am saved! I am
saved! Earth and hell can-not de-stroy, I am saved! I am
saved! Child of God and heir of heav'n, I am saved! I am

saved! Since the Lord hath set me free, Broke the chains that once en-
saved! Tho' my bark be tem-pest tost' In this faith the storms are
saved! Once it scorned the home a-bove, Heart of mine by sin de-
saved! Once the downward path I trod, On-ly earth-ly things I

slaved, Now and thro' e-ter-ni-ty, I am saved! I am saved!
braved; None of His were ev-er lost, I am saved! I am saved!
praved: Now 'tis filled with Je-sus' love; I am saved! I am saved!
craved, Now my heart is fixed on God; I am saved! I am saved!

CHORUS.

I am saved, oh, I am saved! Thanks to Him who died for me, I am saved, oh, I am saved! Now and thro' e - ter - ni - ty.

ROOM IN THE HEART OF JESUS.

Words arranged.

D. B. TOWNER.

1. There is room in the heart of Je - sus, For the
2. There is room in the heart of Je - sus, And He
3. There is room in the heart of Je - sus, Yes, there's

wea - ry, and worn, and sad; There is room in the heart of
com - eth in grace to all; With a mes - sage of full for-
room, come and find it true, Why in sin will you long - er

Je - sus, And a wel - come to make them glad.
give - ness, With a sweet and a lov - ing call.
wan - der? Come, oh, come, while He calls for you.

CHORUS.

There is room,........ There is room,........ There is
There is room, There is room,

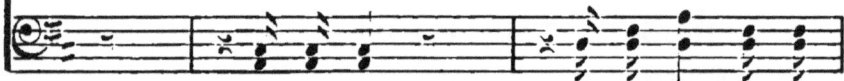

room in the heart of Je - sus, There is room,........ There is
There is room,

room,........ There is room in His heart for thee.
There is room,

F. R. HAVERGAL.   J H. ROSECRANS.

1. Light aft-er dark-ness, Gain aft-er loss, Strength aft-er wea-ri-ness,
2. Sheaves after sow-ing, Sun aft-er rain, Sight aft-er mys-ter-y,
3. Near aft-er dis-tant, Gleam aft-er gloom, Love aft-er lone-li-ness,

Crown aft-er cross, Sweet aft-er bit-ter, Song aft-er sigh,
Peace aft-er pain, Joy aft-er sor-row, Calm aft-er blast,
Life aft-er tomb; Aft-er long ag-o-ny, Rapt-ure of bliss;

CHORUS.

Home aft-er wandering, Praise aft-er cry. ⎫
Rest aft-er weariness, Sweet rest at last. ⎬ Now comes the weeping,
Right was the pathway Lead-ing to this. ⎭

Repeat pp.

Then the glad reaping; Now comes the la-bor hard, Then the re-ward.

BENEATH THY CROSS.

Words selected.　　　　　　　　　　　　　　　　W. J. Baltzell. Arr.

1. Beneath the cross I lay me down, And mourn to see Thy
2. The rage of Sa - tan and of sin, Of foes with-out, and
3. Se - cure from harm beneath Thy shade, Here death and hell shall
4. Oh, un - mo - lest - ed hap-py rest! Where in - ward fears are

blood - y crown; Love drops in blood from ev - 'ry vein; Love
foes with-in, Shall ne'er my conquering soul re - move, Or
ne'er in - vade, Nor Si - nai, with its thund'ring noise, Shall
all suppressed; Here I shall love, and live se - cure, And

Chorus.

is the spring of all Thy pain.
from Thy cross or from Thy love.
e'er disturb my hap - pier joys.
pa - tient- ly my cross en - dure.
} Beneath Thy cross, oh, Christ, I'll

stay,...... And speed my lov-ing hours a - way: I'll shout and
I'll stay,

sing I'm free, I'm free,...... Since on the cross He died for me.
I'm free,

YES, TO THE UTTERMOST.

Rev. E. G. WESLEY.   D. B. TOWNER.

1. Will Je - sus now save a poor sin - ner like me, Who has
2. Does Je - sus in - vite a poor sin - ner like me, All un -
3. Does Je - sus yet love a poor sin - ner like me, As He
4. Oh, tell me! my heart is in an - guish to - night, O - ver -
5. Lord Je - sus, I come, as I am in my sin; At Thy

wan-dered in dark-ness and shame; Will Je - sus for-give a poor
wor - thy, re - bell - ious, de - filed; Will Je - sus re - ceive a poor
sees of my guilt, the dark stain; Will Je - sus ac - cept a poor
whelmed by its sor - row and fear; Will Je - sus give life, if I
cross, neath Thy blood will I rest, I hast - en to Thee, as I

Ad lib.

sin - ner like me; Will He hear if I ask in His name?
sin - ner like me; If I come, will He make me His child?
sin - ner like me; Is it true, that for me He was slain?
seek Him to - night; To my soul will the Sav - ior draw near?
am in my sin, Thou hast saved, I am Thine, I am blest.

YES, TO THE UTTERMOST.

CHORUS.

Yes, ... to the ut - ter-most, Yes, ... to the
Yes, Je - sus saves to the ut - ter-most, Yes, Je-sus saves to the

ut - ter-most, This is the word of God, sure - ly 'tis true;

Yes, ... to the ut - ter-most, Yes, ... to the
Yes, Je-sus saves to the ut - ter-most, Yes, Je - sus saves to the

ut - ter - most, Je - sus, the Sav - ior, will save e - ven you.

HE PLANS MY LIFE.

[The second tenor may be sung as a solo.

C. E. BRECK.   D. B. TOWNER.

1. Re-joice, my soul, be not cast down, Bid all thy fears to cease,
2. I can-not see one step beyond, And would not if I could,
3. He bids me take no anxious load, He will my burdens bear;
4. Oh, nev-er let my heart re-bel, What-ev-er be my lot,

Since God will un-der-take for me, And gives His joy and peace. He
But God hath said all things shall work Together for my good; Then
So at His feet I lay them down, Thankful to leave them there; My
Since Je-sus do-eth all things well, I'll trust and murmur not: So

knows the present and the past, He knows what is to be (is to be);
glad-ly will I trust the love Of such a friend as He (such as He),
life is safe in His dear hands, Contented, glad and free (glad and free),
when my way seems dark as night, I know that God can see (God can see);

And I may safe-ly trust in Him Who plans my life for me.
And bless His wise om-nip-o-tence, Who plans my life for me.
For like a child I trust in Him Who plans my life for me.
And He is lead-ing me a-right Who plans my life for me.

SAVIOR, BREATHE A BLESSING.

LENK. Arr.

1. Sav - ior, breathe an ev - 'ning, bless-ing, Ere re - pose our
2. Tho' the night be dark and drear - y, Darkness can - not

spir - its seal; Sin and want we come con-fessing Thou canst
hide from Thee; Thou art He who, nev - er weary, Watcheth

Tho' destruction walk a-

save, and Thou canst heal, Tho' de-struc-tion walk around us,
where Thy peo - ple be; Should swift death this night o'ertake us,

Tho' destruction walk a-

round us, Tho' the, etc.

Tho' the ar-rows near us fly, An-gel guards from Thee sur-
And our couch become our tomb, May the morn in heav'n a-

round us, Tho' the, etc.

p   *f*   *ff*

round us, We are safe if Thou art nigh, If Thou art nigh.
wake us, Clad in light and deathless bloom, And deathless bloom.

GOOD NIGHT.

ELLA LAUDER.   D. B. TOWNER.

1. Lov - ing word that's night-ly whispered O'er each ti - ny
2. When the toils of day are o - ver, Friend to friend bids
3. Gen - tly whispered by the dy - ing, At the fad - ing
4. Some good-night will be the last one, When our days of

trun-dle - bed, While a moth- er's ben - e - dic - tion Falls up-
soft good-night, Praying that the com-ing mor - row Be with
of the day, Ent'ring in up - on the shin-ing Of the
earth are o'er, When we reach the shin-ing por - tal, And earth's

CHORUS.

on the sleeper's head.
heaven's blessing bright.
heav'nly light for aye.
twi-lights are no more.
    Loving good-night, ten -der good-night,

GOOD NIGHT.

Sweet words of part - ing, good - night: Parting is on - ly,

on - ly for night; Meet-ing will come with the light, (good-night.)

pp

pp

THE REAPER AND THE FLOWERS.

HENRY W. LONGFELLOW.   D. B. TOWNER.

1. There is a reaper, whose name is Death, And with his sick-le keen,
2. "Shall I have naught that is fair," said he, "have naught but the bearded grain?
3. He gazed at the flow'rs with tearful eyes, He kissed their drooping leaves,
4. "My Lord has need of these flowerets gay," The reaper said and smiled,
5. "They shall all bloom in fields of light, Transplanted by my care;
6. And the mother gave, in tears and pain, The flowers she most did love;
7. Oh, not in cruelty, not in wrath, The Reaper came that day;

He reaps the bearded grain at a breath, And the flow'rs that grow between;
Tho' the breath of these flow'rs is sweet to me, I will give them back a-gain."
It was for the Lord of Paradise, He bound them in his sheaves.
Dear tokens of the earth are they, Where He was once a child.
And saints, upon their garments white, These sa-cred blos-soms wear.'
She knew she should find them all again In the fields of light a-bove.
'Twas an angel visited the green earth, And took the flow'rs a-way.

I HEARD THE VOICE OF JESUS. 97

Melody in the first Bass.

HORATIUS BONAR   D. B. TOWNER.

1. I heard the voice of Je - sus say, "Come un-to me and rest:
2. I heard the voice of Je - sus say, "Be - hold, I free - ly give
3. I heard the voice of Je - sus say, "I am this dark world's light;

Lay down, thou weary one, lay down Thy head up - on my breast!"
The liv - ing wa - ter, thirst-y one, Stoop down, and drink, and live!"
Look un - to Me, thy morn shall rise, And all thy day be bright!"

I came to Je - sus as I was—Wea-ry and worn and sad;
I came to Je - sus, and I drank Of that life - giv-ing stream;
I looked to Je - sus, and I found In Him my star, my sun;

I found in Him a rest - ing-place, And He has made me glad.
My thirst was quenched, my soul revived, And now I live in Him.
And in that light of life I'll walk Till trav'ling days are done.

ARISE! QUICKLY ARISE!

(Acts 12: 6-10.)

N. B. S. N. B. SARGENT. Arr.

1. An an - gel came to Pe - ter one night, As he
2. The chains fell off as quick - ly he rose The
3. The i - ron gate swung o - pen that night, And
4. The an - gel comes to you oft - en - times, Your
slept in the pris - on drear; "A - rise up quickly!" were
sum - mons to o - bey, And wond'ring, trembling, he
Pe - ter went bold - ly through; Now list - en, friend, what-
coun - sel - or and guide; Oh, hear his voice, and
words that fell On the start - led pris - 'ner's ear.
fol - lowed on, As the an - gel led the way.
ev - er your chain, There is free-dom this night for you.
fol - low him, And the gate will o - pen wide.
CHORUS.
A - rise! quick - ly a - rise! Ye pris - 'ners in

Copyright, 1894, by D. B Towner.

bond-age to sin, There's a life that is bet-ter than

this for you, And now is the time to be-gin.

KEEP RANK.

L. M. B. BATEMAN.

D. B. TOWNER.

1. Keep rank, keep rank, make Je-sus King, His ban - ner
2. Keep rank, nor give one tho't to fear, Your lead - er's
3. Keep rank, the strife will soon be done, The glo - rious

on the breezes fling, Come ral - ly round His standard high, And
or - ders, on - ly bear, And mid the bat - tle smoke and din, Press
vic - t'ry soon be won, Triumphant then thro' heav'n shall ring, Keep

CHORUS.

in His name all foes de - fy.
on, His might-y cause to win.
rank, keep rank, make Jesus King.
} Keep rank, keep rank, make Je-sus

King,   Tho' foes as-sail on ev - 'ry hand, At
Keep rank,

right and left tho' ma-ny fall, Close up the lines, Oh, hear the call,

And round your colors nobly stand, Keep rank, keep rank, make Jesus King.

DRIFTING AWAY.

C. L. Shacklock.   D. B. Towner.

DUET & CHORUS.

1. They are drift-ing a-way on the sea of life, On its
2. Let the bea-con of hope thro' the dark-ness shine, For the
3. They are drift-ing a-way from the light of home, They are

foam-ing bil-lows tossed, They are wea-ry and faint with the
wand'rers of the wave, There is mer-cy and love in the
los-ing man-hood's pride, They are wrecking their hopes for the

CHORUS.

fruit-less strife, In a mo-ment they'll be lost.
Fount di-vine, All the wrecked of earth to save.   Drift-ing a-
life to come, They are drifting with the tide.

way,...... . Drift-ing a-way,........ They are drift-ing
Drifting a-way,   Drift-ing a-way,

Copyright, 1894, by D. B. Towner.

far-ther and far-ther a - way,...... Far-ther and far-ther a-

Drift - ing a - way,........ Drift-ing a - way,........
way, Drifting a - way, Drifting a - way,

Rit. ad lib.

They are drifting far - ther and far - ther a - way......
They are drifting farther away, Farther away.

FLEE AS A BIRD.

MARY S. B. DANA.　　　　　　　　　Spanish.

SOLO or QUARTET.

1. Flee as a bird to your mount-ain, Thou who art wea-ry of
2. He will protect thee for - ev - er, Wipe ev - 'ry fall - ing
3. Come then, to Je-sus thy Sav - ior, He will re-deem thee from

sin;   Go to the clear flowing fountain, Where you may wash and be
tear; He will forsake thee, oh, nev - er, Sheltered so ten-der-ly
sin;   Bless with the sense of His fa - vor, Make thee all glorious with-

clean; Fly, for th'aveng-er is near thee, Call, and the Savior will
there! Haste, then, the hours are fly - ing, Spend not the moments in
in.   Call, for the Sav - ior is near thee, Wait-ing in mer-cy to

hear thee, He   on His bo - som will bear thee, O
sigh - ing, Cease from your sor - row and cry - ing, The
hear thee, And by His pres - ence to cheer thee, O

thou who art wea-ry of sin, O thou who art wea-ry of sin.
Sav - ior will wipe ev-'ry tear, The Sav - ior will wipe ev-'ry tear.
thou who art wea-ry of sin, O thou who art wea-ry of sin.

O WONDROUS CROSS.

C. L. Eby.   A. F. Myers. By per.

1. Up-on the cross........ my Sav-ior died,........ And for my
2. I sought at length....... His par-don free,........ I gained at
3. I'll sing His pow'r....... while I have breath,...... I'll sing in

1. Up-on the cross   my Savior died,

sins.... was cru-ci-fied;.... His love so great,.... how can it
once..... sweet lib-er-ty:...... E'en now, by faith,.... I claim Him
glo - ry aft-er death;.... Redeemed, redeemed,.... I know I'm

And for my sins   was crucified;   His love so great,

be,........ My Savior died,........ yes, died for me?........
mine,...... I am re-deemed........ by grace di-vine........
free,....... I've peace with God,...... and lib-er-ty.........

how can it be,   My Savior died,   yes, died for me?

CHORUS.

O wondrous cross, ... O Cal-va-ry,......... My longing
O wondrous cross,   O Cal-va-ry,

O WONDROUS CROSS.

eyes.......look up to thee,...... O wondrous cross,.... where Jesus
My longing eyes   look up to thee,   O wondrous cross,

died,........ And for my sins.......... was cru - ci - fied.
where Je-sus died,   And for my sins

ROW ME OVER THE STREAM.

Rev. J. H. Sammis.   D. B. Towner.

1. Boat - man, my spir - it is yearn - ing, There in the
2. There the be - lov - ed are wait - ing, Gath - ered to
3. Sad were the days of our part - ing, Long were the
4. Boat - man, de - lay not thy com - ing, Speed - i - ly

glo - ry to be; There where the Lord is pre - par - ing
Je - sus be - fore; Wait - ing in glo - ry to greet me,
years that are flown, Brief is the journey be - fore me,
fer - ry me o'er; Sweet is the wel-come a - wait - ing,

Copyright owned by D. B. Towner.

CHORUS.

Wel-come and bless-ing for me.
Where we shall sev-er no more.
Bear me a - way to my own.
There on the hap - pi - er shore. Row me o - ver, row me o - ver,
O - ver, o - ver,
Row me o - ver, row me o - ver,

Boat - man, row me o - ver the stream, Loved ones are

wait-ing to greet my com - ing, Row me o - ver the stream.

IS MY NAME THERE?

Rev. G. W. Crofts.   D. B. Towner.

1. There is a Book.... of Life a - bove,....Where all the good....
2. Its pages shine....with heav'nly light, Undimmed by clouds...
3. O Book of Life....bought with that blood, More dear than gold..
4. Re-deem-er mine,....to Thee I look,....Oh, let me now.......

1. There is a Book of Life above, Where all the good

and ho-ly are;........ The record of......... redeeming
of pain and care,....... O bliss-ful realm......where falls no
or jew-els rare;....... O cru - el nails, ... O cross of
Thy mer-cy share,...... And read at last, ... within Thy

and ho-ly are; The record of

love;........ Is my name there?.... Is my name there?.....
night,....... Is my name there?.... Is my name there?.....
wood,....... Is my name there?.... Is my name there?.....
Book,—..... De-light-ful thought!.. My own name there.....

redeeming love; Is my name there? Is my name there?

CHORUS.

Is my name there? Is my name there? Within the Book of Life so fair;

Rit. ad lib.

O Lamb of God, hear Thou my pray'r, And write my name forever there.

108   MY FAITH CLINGS TO JESUS.

FRANK GOULD.   J. R. SWENEY. By per.

1. My faith is cling-ing to the cross so dear; All my care
2. Be - neath the shad-ow of the Rock so high, Still I rest,
3. I hear the mu - sic of the an-gels bright, O'er the sea,

Leav-ing there, For well I know that He, my Lord, is near;
Safe and blest, While faith beholds, with calm and steadfast eye,
Call - ing me, While faith looks up be-yond the gates of light,

CHORUS.

He who knows my ev - 'ry fear. }
Heaven's joys that nev - er die. } What tho' a - round me
Where at home I soon shall be. }

dark clouds may roll! Faith clings to Je - sus, anch-or of my soul;.... Oh, how my Sav-ior loves me! Praise, praise His ho-ly

name! Break forth, my heart, my tongue, His mighty love pro-claim!

OH, WHERE WILL YOU BE?

Rev. J. H. Sammis.   D. B. Towner.

1. Oh, where will you be   when e - ter - ni - ty dawns;
2. Oh, where will you be   when the Judge is en-throned,
3. Oh, where will you be   when He bids them de - part,
4. Oh, where will you be   while e - ter - ni - ties roll;

When Christ un - to   judg-ment re - turn - eth   a - gain,
And   sin - ners as - sem - ble be - fore Him to know
And   forth from His pres - ence the sons of   de - spair
In   man - sions of   glo - ry   and end - less de - light,

OH, WHERE WILL YOU BE?

And clad in the flesh from their cav - erns of gloom,
The is - sues of life and the fate of the soul,
Shall each to his pris - on e - ter - nal de - scend?
Or far from the smile and the joy of the Lord?

Shall is - sue at last, all the chil - dren of men?
Its sad con-dem - na - tion; its por - tion of woe?
Will you, oh, will you in their mis - er - y share?
O sin - ner, de - cide it, de-cide it to - night.

CHORUS.

Then where will you be, broth - er, where will you be?

Oh, where will you be when e - ter - ni - ty dawns?

THINE ALONE.

Rev. J. H. Sammis.   R. T. Owen.

1. By grace redeemed thro' Thy blood, O Lord, I am Thine, Thine a-lone:
2. I am dead to sin, but a-live to Thee, I am Thine, Thine a-lone:
3. Thy name I love, and Thy service choose, I am Thine, Thine a-lone;
4. What peace it brings to my heart to know I am Thine, Thine a-lone;

Oh, may my will with Thine own accord, I am Thine, Thine a - lone.
Thy bonds are glo- ri- ous lib - er - ty, I am Thine, Thine a - lone.
Now make me meet for my Master's use, I am Thine, Thine a - lone.
To watch and wait, or to will and do, I am Thine, Thine a - lone.

CHORUS.

Lord, Thou hast bought me, I am not my own; Thy

word of grace to my heart is whis-per-ing, Thine, Thine a - lone.

Copyright, 1894, by D. B. Towner.

112 SOFTLY NOW THE LIGHT OF DAY.

KREUTZER.

p Adagio.

Soft - ly now the light of day Fades up-on our
Free from care, from la - bor free, Lord, we would com-

sight a - way,)
mune with Thee; ∫ Soon for us the light of day...... Soon for us the light of

day Shall for - ev - er pass a - way,
Shall for - ev - er pass a - way, pass a - way,

Rit.

Dolce. *Tempo ad lib.*

Then from sin and sor-row free, Take us Lord to dwell with Thee,

Then from sin and sor-row free . . . .
Then from sin and sor-row free,

Take us, Lord, to dwell with Thee, ...
Take us, Lord, to dwell with Thee,

O take us, take us, Lord, to dwell with Thee,
O take us, Lord, to dwell, to dwell with Thee,

O Lord, to dwell with Thee, O Lord, to dwell with Thee!

HE REDEEMED ME.

E. A. H.

E. A. HOFFMAN. Arr.

1. I praise the wondrous love of God, The wondrous love of God to me,
2. I had no mer-it of my own, My need I made my on-ly plea,
3. For this I praise the Lord to-day, That love so in-fi-nite and free,
4. He ransomed me, He ransomed me, Such love and grace I now proclaim;

Which moved Him to redeem with blood My soul on Cal-va-ry.
Yet moved by His a-maz-ing grace, He pardoned e-ven me.
Should stoop to bless a fall-en man, And ran-som e-ven me.
He sealed my par-don on the tree, Oh, glo-ry to His name.

CHORUS

He redeemed me, Oh, glory to His name! He redeemed me, His grace I will proclaim,

For His love and grace are evermore the same, Hal-le-lu-jah to His name!

Copyright, 1894, by D. B. Towner.

THAT BEAUTIFUL LAND.

May be sung as a duet by 1st and 2d tenors.

F. A. F. WHITE.   MARK M. JONES. By per.

1. I have heard of a land On a far a - way strand,
2. There are ev - er - green trees That bend low in the breeze,
3. There's a home in that land, At the Fa - ther's right hand;

In the Bi - ble the sto - ry is told, Where
And their fruit-age is bright-er than gold; There are
There are man-sions whose joys are un - told, And per-

cares nev - er come, Nev - er dark - ness nor gloom, And
harps for our hands, In that fair - est of lands, And
en - ni - al spring, Where the birds ev - er sing, And

CHORUS.

noth-ing shall ev - er grow old.
noth-ing shall ev - er grow old.   } In that beau - ti - ful
noth ing can ev - er grow old.

land On the far a - way strand, No storms with their

blasts ev - er frown; The streets, I am told, Are paved with pure

gold, And the sun it shall nev - er go down.

THE REST BEYOND.

N. E. B.

N. E. BYERS. Arr.

1. In the Book there is a sto - ry, Oft in childhood told to me,
2. Of earth's toil-ing are you wea-ry? Sweetly lean on Je-sus' breast:
3. No more sor-row, care or sigh-ing, Freed from mortal fear and pain:
4. Then cheer up, my fainting brother, Soon will come the promised rest:

Of   a home prepared in glo - ry Where the pure in heart shall be.
Tho' the way is sometimes drear-y, There remains a peace-ful rest.
In the land be-yond the dy-ing, We with Christ shall ev-er reign.
Follow Christ, seek not an-oth - er, He will lead to mansions blest.

CHORUS.

There's a   home...... prepared in glo - ry,   Safe from
There's a home,   a   home prepared in glory,

earth - - ly flame and flood;........ I be - lieve...... the
Safe from earth - ly danger, flame and flood;   I be-lieve

grand old sto - ry;   Sweet rest for the children of God.
the   sto - ry, grand old sto-ry;

ASHAMED OF JESUS.

JOSEPH GRIGG.   D. B. TOWNER.

1. Je - sus, and shall it ever be,   A mor-tal man ashamed of Thee,
2. A-shamed of Je-sus! sooner far   Let ev'ning blush to own a star;
3. A-shamed of Je-sus! yes, I may   When I've no guilt to wash away,
4. Till then, nor is my boasting vain,   Till then, I boast a Savior slain,

Ashamed of Thee, whom angels praise, Whose glories shine thro' endless days?
He sheds the beams of light divine O'er this be-nighted soul of mine.
No tear to wipe, no good to crave, No fear to quell, no soul to save.
And oh, may this my glo-ry be, That Christ is not ashamed of me.

CHORUS.

Ashamed of Je - sus!   that dearest friend,
Ashamed of Je - sus! that dear friend, ...

On whom my hopes   of heav'n depend,
On whom my hopes.......... of heav'n de - pend,.........

No, when I blush,
be this my shame,

No, when I blush,.......... be this my shame,........

That I no more
re-vere His name.

That I no more.......... re-vere His name..........

THE GRACIOUS CALL.

ANNA L. BARBAULD.

Arranged for this work.

1. "Come," said Je-sus' sacred voice, "Come, and make my paths your choice;
2. Ye who, tossed on beds of pain, Seek for ease, but seek in vain,
3. Hith-er come, for here is found Balm that flows for ev-'ry wound;

I will guide you to your home: Wea-ry pil-grim, hith-er come."
Ye, by fierc-er an-guish torn, In remorse for guilt who mourn,
Peace that ev-er shall en-dure, Rest e-ter-nal, sa-cred, sure.

120 SEND THE WORD.

A. R. CAREY.   D. B. TOWNER.

1. Have the mill-ions been told of the ban - quet That the
2. Have they heard what the King waits to give them? Spread the
3. Have they heard of the life-bloom im - mor - tal? Deathless
4. Do they know how this boun - ty was pur - chased, How the

King in His pal - ace has spread; Bread of life, flowing draughts,
news, lest the gifts they should spurn; Rich pos-ses-sions where naught
pleas - ure for pain He will give, Strength to walk mid the bow'rs
blood of the Lamb bought it all? Tell them now, for He longs

that will ev - er Keep all want from the souls that are fed?
can in - vade them, If they'll give but their hearts in re - turn.
and the fount - ains, If they'll turn to the Heal - er and live.
to be - stow it On the souls that will fol - low His call.

CHORUS.

Send the word,   Send the word,
Send the word,.. .... Till the mill - ions have heard

SEND THE WORD.

It is on - ly a lit - tle way to go,
a lit - tle way to go,

Bid them come,
Bid them come............. To the King's pal - ace home,
Bid them come,

Just a - cross where the storms nev - er blow.
where the storms nev - er blow.

HE AROSE.

Geo. C. Hugg.
Slowly.
Geo. C. Hugg.

1. Low - ly en-tombed He lay, My bless- ed Sav - ior;
2. Vain - ly they watch Him now, My bless- ed Sav - ior;
3. Burst - ing the seal He rose, My bless- ed Sav - ior;

By permission.

Wait - ing the promised day, My pre - cious Lord.
Sure - ly He'll keep His vow, My pre - cious Lord.
Scat - t'ring His arm - ed foes, My pre - cious Lord.

CHORUS.

Up from the tomb He a - rose! And in tri - umph
He a-rose!

vanquished all His foes, He a - rose a vic - tor o'er the
all His foes,

realms of night, And He reigns for-ev - er with His saints in light, He a

HE AROSE.

rose, He a-rose He a-rose Vic-tor o - ver all His foes.
He a-rose, He a-rose

ROCK OF AGES.

TOPLADY. Arr. by D. A. NIEL.

1. Rock of A - ges, cleft for me, Let me hide my -
2. Could my tears for - ev - er flow, Could my zeal no
3. While I draw this fleet - ing breath, When my eyes shall

self in Thee; Let the wa - ter and the blood From Thy
lan - guor know, These for sin could not a - tone; Thou must
close in death, When I rise to worlds un-known, And be-

wounded side which flowed, Be of sin.......... the double cure,
save, and Thou a-lone; In my hand........ no price I bring;
hold Thee on Thy throne, Rock of A - - - - ges, cleft for me,

Be of sin the double cure,

Save me from.......... its guilt and pow'r. Be of sin
Sim-ply to............ Thy cross I cling. In my hand
Let me hide.......... my-self in Thee. Rock of A - - - -

Save me from its   guilt and pow'r.   Be of sin
its guilt and pow'r.

Ad lib.

the doub-le cure, Save me from   its guilt and pow'r.
no price I bring, Sim-ply to   Thy cross I cling.
ges, cleft for me, Let me hide   my-self in Thee.

the doub-le cure,   Save me from its guilt and pow'r.

JESUS, THE SINNER'S FRIEND.

A. W. M.   Arr. by J. H. ROSECRANS.

1. { Je-sus, the sinner's friend, I look to Thee;
   { Draw near and bless me now; O speak to me! Come, and Thyself reveal.
2. { To Thee, I turn mine eyes, Thou bleeding Lamb;
   { Oh, shine within my heart, And make me calm; For Thee my spirit cries,
3. { Oh, let Thy im-age fair By pow'r di - vine,
   { Be per-fect - ed in me, Thou bless-ed One; Teach me Thy will to do.

Come, and my spirit heal; My soul cries out for Thee, Cries out for Thee.
And without Thee it dies; Hear now the pray'r I make, The pray'r I make.
Each day my journey thro', And make me wholly Thine, Yes, whol-ly Thine.

BLESSED IS HE THAT READETH. 125

C. S. COLBURN.

Bless-ed, bless-ed, bless - ed, Bless-ed is he that readeth, and

they that hear the word, the word of the Lord; For He saith un-to you,

He saith un - to you, Tho' your sins be as scar - let, They shall

be as white as snow, Tho' they be red like crimson, They shall be as
They shall be as

Copyright, 1894, by D. B. Towner.

wool;   so loved the world,
wool; For God so loved the world,   That He gave His on-ly

His on - ly Son to   die, to die, That who - so - ev - er be -
Son

lieveth on Him Should not perish, should not perish, But have everlasting

life, But have ever-lasting life, But have ev-er-last - ing   life.

INDEX.

Titles in SMALL CAPS—First lines in Roman.

INDEX.—*Concluded.*